Tartar Treachery

The Inside Story on How International
Bankers, Communist China, and The Vatican
Collaborated to Advance a Centuries Old Plan
for a New World Order

By Susan Bradford

(c) 2021

Tartary

If I were Lord of Tartary
Myself, and me alone
My bed should be of ivory
Of beaten gold my throne
And in my court should peacocks flaunt
And in my forests tigers haunt
And in my pools great fishes slant
Their fins athwart the sun.

If I were Lord of Tartary
Trumpeters every day
To all my meals should summon me
And in my courtyards bray
And in the evening lamps should shine
Yellow as honey, red as wine
While harp, and flute, and mandolin
Made music sweet and gay.

If I were Lord of Tartary
I'd wear a robe of beads
White, and gold, and green they'd be;
And small and thick as seeds;
And ere should wane the morning star,
I'd don my robe and scimitar.
And zebras seven should draw my car
Through Tartary's dark glades.

Lord of the fruits of Tartary.
Her rivers silver-pale!
Lord of the hills of Tartary.
Glen, thicket, wood, and dale!
Her flashing stars, her scented breeze,
Her trembling lakes, like foamless seas,
Her bird-delighting citron-trees,
In every purple vale!

Walter de La Mare

Table of Contents

Books by This Author

ROYAL BLOOD LIES:
The Inside Story on How The Rothschilds Took Over the British Monarchy, Purged Royals, Created Puppet Leaders, Waged Revolutions, Corrupted Morals and Institutions, Plundered Wealth, Created False Realities, and Pitted Nations, Societies, and Peoples Against Each Other in a Ruthless, Megalomaniacal Quest for World Domination

FL33C3D:
Elon Musk, The Green New Deal, and
The Coming Technocracy as Revealed
through The Oklahoma Indian Land Scam

THE SHADOW DRAGON:
The Inside Story Behind Donald Trump's
Struggle to Derail The Deep State

THE FULL COURT PRESS:
How The Bush Administration Managed
The Media through Embedded Reporters, Talking Points,
Black Lists, Intimidation, Back Channels, and Clever PR
(Foreword by Senior CBS Foreign Correspondent Tom Fenton)

LYNCHED!
The Shocking Story on How the Political Establishment
Manufactured a Scandal to Have Republican
Superlobbyist Jack Abramoff Removed from Power

THE TRIBES THAT ROCKEFELLER BUILT:
The Inside Story on How Big Oil and Industry
are Working with and through The Federal Government
and Indian Tribes to Shore up Markets

THE UNITED CHURCH OF HEIST:
How Barack Obama and The Ecumenicists
Transformed The United Church of Christ
into a Political Machine for The Democratic Party

THE SECOND AMERICAN REVOLUTION:
How The Bolsheviks Waged and Lost
The Second American Revolution

UNMASKED: THE CORONAVIRUS STORY:
The Nauseating Truth behind The Global Quest
to Bring The World to Heel, Destroy Nationalism,
and Undermine The Trump Presidency through Fake Scandals,
Simulated Pandemics, Junk Science, Political Puppets,
Brazen Extortion, and Rapacious Money Grabs

About The Author

Susan Bradford is an investigative journalist, public speaker, and author. She has appeared on *The Jeff Rense Show, Ickonic, The Ritchie Allen Show, Business Game Changes with Sarah Westall, One Radio News Network with Patrick Timpone, The Tin Foil Hat Show with Sam Tripoli, Dublin Radio, Erskine Radio, The Charlie Ward Show, The Mel K Show, Making Sense of the Madness, Intelligence Briefing, Down the Rabbit Hole, The Ripple Effect podcast, One Radio News Network, The Charles Moscowitz Show*, the BBC, *The Lazarus Initiative with Sacha Stone*, and elsewhere. Her articles have been featured in the Capital Resource Center's *Institutional Trends, The European Review, UN Vision, Washington Times, Global News, Associated Press, City News Service,* and numerous blogs. She also appeared in a documentary on the Great Reset directed by Paul Wittenberger.

She holds a BA in English from UC Irvine and am MA in International Relations from the University of Essex. She has worked as writer for KNX (CBS) news radio, reporter for City News Service, production assistant for the PBS Red Car Film Project, editor and foreign correspondent for the European Review, producer for Fox News Channel, assignments editor for the Voice of America, and speech writer for Korean Ambassador Sung Chul Yang and speech writer for UK Shadow Foreign Secretary Michael Howard.

www.susanbradford.org

The Devil's Greatest Trick

The devil's greatest trick was convincing the world he didn't exist. What if we could trace his origins to the land of Tartary? Not only could we know that the devil does, in fact, exist, but we could unlock his secrets, understand the strategies he has used to confound humanity, and free ourselves from his power. We could also understand the devil's blinding rage against Jesus Christ.

Jesus established the divine right (rite) to rule, which, in turn, fortified God's dominion on Earth, a development that did not go over well with those who sought to play God.

The divine right (rite) to rule was first challenged by the Vatican which attempted to claim God's temporal authority over humanity through St. Peter. The powerful merchant families who controlled the Vatican weren't interested in serving God's kingdom, in so much as they wanted it run it themselves. They could never legitimately claim the divine right (rite) to rule, and so they did what they thought was the next best thing – they forged alliances with the dark forces of Tartary to establish their own kingdom. You might say they cut a proverbial deal with the devil, who promised them all the wealth, power, and decadent pleasures they could ever want as long as they served him.

As *1 John 5:19* affirms, "the whole world lies in the power of the evil one." Through reason, magic, rituals, and deception, the aspiring rulers would attempt to claim God's authority for themselves. If only they could bury the true story of Jesus, reinvent themselves as Gods on earth, and convince humanity to worship them, they just might reach the elusive status of Jesus.

The alliances forged between the Vatican and China would become the basis for the New World Order through which they sought rule the world with the devils from the deep recesses of Tartary. In the process, they would create Hell on Earth and fulfill Biblical prophecy. These would-be rulers were merely inventions of tradition, wannabes, and frauds. They did not legitimately hold the power that they claimed, and their wealth was mostly stolen. The battle between good and evil was on. You could say that it was Biblical.

I.
The Lion, The Witch, and The Wardrobe

While attempting to debunk Christianity, C.S. Lewis was "surprised by joy" to stumble upon powerful truths hidden in plain sight. The first book in his acclaimed *Chronicles of Narnia* children's series, *The Lion, The Witch, and The Wardrobe,* was warmly received by literary critics who praised its Christian themes, particularly Lewis' portrayal of Aslan, a noble lion who sacrificed his life so that others could live.

Anyone who thought the *Chronicles* were Christian novels missed the point entirely. The parallels between the symbolism in his books and Christianity were mere happenstance. What few appreciated is that Lewis was actually encoding the secrets British and European elites and the Vatican had acquired from Central Asia which traced to Buddhism, Confucianism, and the Egyptian mystery schools. The symbolism was as clear as day for the initiated, accounting for the runaway success of his books.

The Lion, The Witch, and The Wardrobe delighted children, with its mythical creatures, wicked witch, and talking animals. The story was set in the middle of war as bombs rained from the sky. The children sought shelter and comfort in a home with a magical wardrobe only to discover that this wardrobe led to a mythical land called Narnia that was presided over by a wicked witch whose evil had metastasized throughout the land.

The children were told that the evil would dissipate once prophecy was fulfilled: "Wrong will be right, when Aslan comes in sight. At the sound of his roar, sorrows will be no more. When he bares his teeth, winter meets its death. And when he shakes his mane, we shall have spring again."

At the time Lewis wrote the series, Europe was aflame with war, and the Great Game was on to corner markets in China. By this point, ruling elites had rejected truth and salvation through Jesus Christ for the rational Enlightenment. What few appreciated is that the Enlightenment that promised liberty, fraternity, and equality was based upon Chinese Buddhist and Confucian principles which sought to enslave mankind under a ruling elite. The initiated understood the true meaning behind the prophecy which conveyed an altogether different meaning to the masses.

Interpreted through the lens of Buddhism, it becomes clear that the lion of Narnia represents the bodhisattva, a Buddha who has achieved a high level of spiritual enlightenment to arrive at the "great awakening," not to be confused with being "born again" in Christianity through Jesus Christ or a baptism. Chinese Buddhists rejected salvation and everlasting life through Jesus for what they thought was better – reincarnation through blood ritual and enlightenment. As a god-king, the bodhisattva sits on a throne.

The "rational Enlightenment" was sold to the West as a replacement for Judaeo-Christianity, that of freeing oneself from the bondage of a nonexistent God so that one could do what was in one's own best interests without having to consult one's conscience.

If each individual were a unique expression of God's infinite greatness, then to deny someone else their free will, to enslave them, and act as their God, was immoral. If God were dead, as Friedrich Nietzsche declared, then morals were irrelevant. Immoral conduct could be justified on grounds that it advanced someone else's interests. The reality elites were creating was one of a Hobbesian *bellum omnium contra omnes*, or a "war of all against all."

The rational Enlightenment was the philosophy of unprincipled opportunists who promoted the politics of envy by portraying those who held wealth as having acquired it unjustly so that envious wannabes could unleash their hordes and claim what they wanted for themselves. War, revolution, barn burning, guillotines, human sacrifice – nothing was off limits to ambitious wannabes stripped of moral restraint. Rational self-interest reduced reality to its cold, hard, cynical essence, to give one the clarity one needed to serve oneself above all others. Without empathy, love, or virtue, people could be reduced to animals for whom anything could be rationally justified.

The poor weren't to be educated, so they could not understand how the wealthy exploited them. After all, empowering the poor with education would not be in the rational self-interest of the rich. Being rationally self-interested meant taking whatever you wanted, even if you had to circumvent the law or harm others to do it. In his Farewell address, America's Founding Father, Gen. George Washington, encouraged his fellow countrymen to avoid foreign entanglements to keep such people off our shores, to prevent them from corrupting a society created of, by, and for a free people of God. As the French philosopher Alexis de Tocqueville observed, America was great because its people were good. Once Americans surrendered their goodness as a godly people, all hell broke loose.

The name "Aslan" codifies the rise of Asian power. For centuries, powerful merchants had partnered with Asian mercenaries to tap markets and establish monopolies in Central Asia. Through these associations, Western merchants acquired the secrets of occult-practicing warlords who lived in palatial mansions laced in gold and jewels. The power the warlords held over subjugated people was envied by power-seeking wannabes. Had they remained true to their Judaeo-Christian traditions, the merchants would have rejected the barbaric practices they observed outright. Based upon the conduct observed at the Vatican, it was clear that remaining virtuous and pleasing to God weren't high among their priorities. The adage, "if you can't beat them, join them," was the order of the day among a merchant class who traded finery, jewels, and occult powers for the survival of humanity.

The second prophecy in the *Lion* is: "When Adam's flesh and Adam's bones sits at Cair Paravel in throne, the evil time will be over and done." Adam first appeared in *Genesis* at the Garden of Eden, which was historically set in Tabriz, Iran/Persia. Here Adam and Eve were presented with the "fruit of knowledge" from a serpent, who represents the spirit of evil. God warns the couple not to accept the fruit of knowledge on penalty of being cast from paradise.

Lewis' statement concerning Adam alludes to the Chinese Buddhist belief that reincarnation is possible through rituals involving flesh and bones. With each reincarnation, one reaches higher stages of enlightenment.

Education and wisdom were prized among Jews and Christians, so God's message in *Genesis* was not to embrace ignorance but refrain from partaking in the fruit of knowledge which leads to spiritual death. The serpent was not offering true wisdom, but knowledge of the occult. Jesus admonished God's people against soothsayers and speaking to the dead.

In the third part of the prophecy, the children learn that the witch will fall "when two Sons of Adam and two Daughters of Eve sit in those four thrones," hinting at a secret known at the Vatican that there were two Jesuses and at least two Marys, all of whom lived at the same time, sources close to the British Monarchy report.

The children also meet a faun by the name of Mr. Tumnus, which appears to be a veiled reference to Tammuz, the false Messiah and reincarnated sun-god (Ba'al) referenced in *Ezekiel 8:14* who is associated with the worship of Nimrod (Osiris) and his illegitimate son, Horus. The myth of Osiris, death, and regeneration is replayed throughout elite circles, referencing the supposed ascension of initiates to God-like status through magic, rituals, and reincarnation. Osiris, Isis, and Horus represent the Trinity. Sometimes the deity is represented as Osiris-Ra to signify that the Father and the Son are one and the same.

The children greet Aslan at a "stone table," or Buddhist altar of stones. The Tibetan Buddhist mantra, "Om Mani padme hum," translates into "the jewel is in the lotus," representing the flower of enlightenment. Within Buddhism, diamonds cut through illusions; rubies honor the Buddha; sapphires promote spiritual enlightenment; and turquoise destroys monsters and celebrates wealth.

The children are told that once the snow melts, the witch's power will fade. In the final battle between good and evil, the witch invokes the "deep magic" from the "dawn of time," alluding to the magic that has been around forever. Aslan is then slain by the witch only to be born again, reflecting the karma-based reincarnation of Buddhism.

In the end, a reincarnated Aslan kills the witch, the snow melts, and the children are crowned kings and queens, reflecting the history of warring nomads in Central Asia who, upon slaughtering their rivals, become Royalty and bodhisattvas. The victors are rewarded with riches, slaves, and the mandate from heaven to rule.

Interestingly, Lewis places the castle of Narnia on a hill overlooking the Great River valley with its East door opening to the sea. The powerful Chinese city which links the Vatican and City of London to China was Shanghai through which the Yangtze River flows into the ocean. Shanghai is associated with great wealth and power, but also great evil and treachery.

In 1863, Jesuit missionaries erected a church in Shanghai at Sheshan West Hill, the location of an abandoned Buddhist temple where royalty came to worship. In 1942, Pope Pius XII ordained the Shanghai Cathedral as a minor basilica. In 1946, the Holy Sea crowned its Madonna. Four years later, *The Lion, The Witch, and The Wardrobe* was published. The Cultural Revolution led by Mao Tse-tung followed soon after. Once Mao assumed power, the cathedral was destroyed, and the Roman Catholic bishop of Shanghai was arrested and imprisoned. The basilica was then placed under the control of the Chinese Patriotic Catholic Association.

Lewis achieved a level of success mirroring that of JK Rowling, the global bestselling author of the *Harry Potter* series who introduced children to magic and witchcraft. During his lifetime, Lewis wrote over 30 books which were translated into 30 languages and featured in dramas, films, and radio and television programs, making him a global superstar. During the World Wars, the Ministry of Information approached him to write articles for the press, but he refused on grounds that he did not wish to "write lies." Instead, he produced religious programming for the BBC which catapulted him into literary superstardom. Having seen a glimpse of the evil that was overtaking humanity, Lewis rationally concluded that Christianity was a force for good in the world and promptly converted to the faith. As Sir Donald Hardman wrote, "The war, the whole of life, everything tended to seem pointless. We needed, many of us, a key to the meaning of the universe. Lewis provided just that."

King George VI recommended Lewis for the honor of Commander of the Order of the British Empire, but the author declined on grounds that he did not wish to be associated with the politics of Britain.

Lewis said he learned "never to trust a papist," but that he made an exception for J.R.R. Tolkien, the author of *The Hobbit* and *The Lord of The Rings* who attempted to write a book linking a fictional "Middle Earth" to "Lord Road," but died before the manuscript could be completed. C.S. Lewis credits Tolkien with opening his eyes to the truth of Christianity. In *Mere Christianity*, Lewis wrote: "A man who was merely a man and said the sort of things Jesus said would not be a great moral teacher. He would either be a lunatic – on the level with the man who says he is a poached egg – or else he would be the Devil of Hell. You must make your choice. Either this man was, and is, the Son of God, or else a madman or something worse. You can shut him up for a fool, you can spit at him and kill him as a demon, or you can fall at his feet and call him Lord and God, but let us not come with any patronizing nonsense about his being a great human teacher. He has not left that open to us. He did not intend to." C.S. Lewis never trusted the Vatican, but he came to understand it.

Worship God or Play God

Buddhism was spreading throughout Central Asia, India, and China before Jesus Christ was even born. Siddhartha Gautama Buddha, the founder of Buddhism, was conceived through a virgin birth in India between the fifth and fourth centuries BCE after his mother, the Queen Maya, received a prophetic dream that the bodhisattva (future Buddha) would enter her womb from heaven.

The ancient Egyptians conceived God as an ancient avian creature named Ra who laid an egg in the Nile River so that he could be born again. Regeneration, or the ability to be born again, became one of the qualifiers for the status of God, as demonstrated by Jesus, bodhisattvas, and Egyptian deities. Osiris, a deity associated with regeneration, was heralded as the Lord of Lords, the God of Gods, and the King of Kings.

Recognized as both God and man, Osiris became the first King of Egypt. Osiris was killed, dismembered, and then tossed into the Nile River. His consort, Isis, avenged the death with Horus, the God of the Sky. Osiris was then resurrected.

During Aristotle's life, the Greeks colonized Egypt, providing ancient Greek philosophers the opportunity to learn the secrets of the Egyptian mystery schools and the occult. The Greek Pharaoh, Alexander the Great, established the library of Alexandria which became one of the largest research institutes in the world, with upwards of over 400,000 papyrus scrolls documenting the secrets.

Ptolemy VIII Physcon, the King of Egypt (184-116 BC) and the grandfather of Roman Emperor Julius Caesar, purged the intellectuals and began the process of destroying the library. Caesar leveled the library entirely in a civil war in 48 BC. Celebrated as Divine Julius, the Roman Emperor challenged the corrupt ruling classes to restore power and rights to the people. As Christianity spread, support for the library dwindled.

Through sacred initiation and bloodline, rulers could claim the divine right (rite) to rule – a right the Pope tried to claim for himself so that the Papacy would have the authority to appoint rulers who answered to a powerful merchant class which controlled the Vatican.

The aspiring ruling class of merchants privately rejected Jesus while finding inspiration in Plato and Aristotle who promoted a world view that rejected God's dominion. Aspiring rulers looked to these philosophers and Central Asia for the "rational Enlightenment" to overthrow Christian Monarchs and replace them with republics that served a powerful merchant class. Plato wasn't interested in having elected officials serve or represent the people, but in having a shadow elite wield influence through them.

The Christians challenged paganism and attempted to establish their own libraries, including, for example, the Theological Library of Caesarea Maritima, the Library of Jerusalem, and a Christian library in Alexandria, so that scholars could explore both paganism and Christianity and learn the divine spark of truth for themselves.

The Greeks were determined to retain the power they had acquired through the occult. Many rejected Christianity and converted to Eastern religions like Islam. Not only did the Ottoman caliphate celebrate Greek culture and institutions, but Sultans and Pashas of Greek ancestry ruled the Muslim Ottoman Empire.

The Central Asian empires extended throughout Turkish territory, creating a confluence of interests among occultists, war lords, and merchants who aspired to conquer Christendom, and ultimately, the world. As French Monarchs would later discover, the Vatican was bankrolling "infidel" attacks against Christian kingdoms while representing itself as the defender of Christianity.

Building upon the myth of Osiris, the Greeks introduced the idea of a Serapis, or Sun God, who was named patron and God of Alexandria with Osiris. A Graeco-Egyptian deity, the Serapis was portrayed as having aspects from both cultures. He was also associated with Hades (Hell) and Dionysus (the God of debauchery).

The Buddhists had acquired knowledge of the Egyptian mystery schools before the Greeks, allowing the occult to spread through India and Central Asia by way of trade. According to renowned British archaeologists, Buddhism dates back to the Persian period of Egypt between 525 to 405 BC. The first direct contact between Egypt and India took place in the third millennium BC. In the seventh century, trade increased after Greek merchants and explorers penetrated Egypt.

It would not be long before what God had established the devil would cast asunder. Within centuries, the Roman Empire crumbled, giving way to a newly formed Byzantine Empire and the Holy Roman Empire, with the former serving as gateway to Central Asia, an area encompassing Egypt, the Mediterranean, and parts of Turkey, and the latter forming a powerful alliance with the Vatican.

Meanwhile, powerful Italian merchants were seeking a means through which they could pursue power under the banner of God's authority, even though they rejected God. The Vatican proved to be the perfect vehicle. Obstructing the ambitions of these merchants was a sacred bloodline and initiation through Jesus which they could never obtain, and so they decided upon the next best thing – that they would *become* God.

Robbing St. Peter to Pay Paul

The Catholic Church was established through the authority of St. Paul, a Jewish disciple of Christ who was among the first two apostles to acknowledge Jesus as "the Christ, the Son of the living God." Jesus recognized that Peter's sentiments were inspired by "my Father, who is in heaven."

"Upon this rock," Jesus said, "I will build my church, and the gates of Hades will not overpower it. I will give you the keys to the Kingdom of Heaven, and whatever you bind on Earth shall have been bound in Heaven, and whatever you lose shall have been lost in Heaven."

Based upon this biblical passage, the Catholic Church maintains that Jesus conferred upon St. Peter and all successive Popes the authority to serve as God's temporal authority on Earth. But far from being holy men, the Catholic Church has been dominated by powerful, often sacrilegious families who used the moral authority of the Church as a cloak for brazen power grabs and plunder. By asserting the authority of Jesus, they ensured they would never be questioned or have to answer for what they did. As head of the Catholic Church, St.

Peter and all Popes who followed after him would be the "chosen one at Babylon," with Babylon referring to Rome.

The first Roman Emperor to formally convert to Christianity was Constantine the Great (306-337 AD). While aggressively rebuffing barbarian invasions from Central Asia, Constantine I strengthened the Empire and introduced gold coins to facilitate trade. He also helped legitimatize the Pope by paying taxes to him in recognition of the papacy's divine authority – a recognition consistent with the Chinese tributary system in which the ruler is entitled to receiving tribute from the ruled by virtue of holding a mandate from heaven. "St. Peter is the Apostle of Jesus of whom Jesus gave His kingdom – therefore (the Pope) will receive taxes," Constantine said.

**Chi Rho: By this symbol
we will conquer.**

The Pope claimed *unam sanctum* – that is, ownership of all souls and their possessions, lives, and destinies on Earth. *Unam sanctam* was formalized in 1302 under a papal bull issued by Pope Boniface VII who declared conversion to Catholicism as a requirement for eternal salvation. Through this bull, the Vatican attempted to claim ownership of all the land, resources, businesses, governments, and people on Earth. Interestingly, a symbol used by the Catholic Church is Emperor Constantine's military standard -- Chi Rho, which means, "by this symbol, we will conquer."

The Vatican's efforts to claim rank over European Monarchs were met with resistance. For example, in his eagerness to assert papal supremacy, Pope Boniface VIII challenged French King Philip IV's efforts to tax Catholic clergy, claiming *unam sanctam,* or "One Holy," and then asserting that only the Vatican held the authority to tax.

The King laughed at the suggestion, advising the Pope that far from being holy, he was a blasphemous, murderous sodomite. After telling the Pope what he thought of him, the King ordered his mercenaries to arrest Monsieur One Holy at his palace at Anagni, leading the Pope to mourn his "Babylonian captivity."

The Vatican had similarly attempted to claim supremacy over British Monarchs by refusing to provide a dispensation to King Henry VIII so that he could divorce Catherine of Aragon and marry Anne Boleyn, the sister of one of his mistresses. The Vatican's decision was likely based upon the fact that the Holy Roman Emperor, Charles V, was the Pope's ally and Catherine's nephew. Therefore it was in the Vatican's interests to retain the marriage to wield influence over the Monarch. King Henry VIII rebuffed the Pope, established the Church of England as separate from the Vatican, and then proceeded to marry Anne Boleyn, who was subsequently executed, or as sources close to the Monarch maintain, staged her own execution so that she could flee to safety.

The Vatican assaults on European Monarchies were unrelenting. As would soon become clear, the Papacy was less interested in saving souls than it was in claiming them as assets. In 800 A.D. the Frankish king of the Holy Roman Empire, Charlemagne, coronated the Pope "Emperor of the Romans," solidifying an alliance between the Franks and the Pope – and the powerful merchants who controlled the Papacy. The Vatican sought to restore the fallen Roman Empire, this time under the control of the power merchant families who had established a foothold in the lucrative markets of Central Asia.

Gone without a Trace

Within the span of a few centuries, the Vatican had come to dominate churches and parishes throughout Europe. Powerful merchant dynasties, like the de Medici family, coalesced around the lagoons of Venice, having amassed a fortune through maritime trade with Central Asia. This was one of many unscrupulous merchant families who formed the Black Nobility, inspiring aware and fear for the ruthless tactics they employed to corner markets and acquire wealth. Rather than pursue commerce based upon good faith, the

Vatican legitimized and provided material support to predatory merchants for whom nothing was sacred. Dirty tricks, false flag operations, extermination events, assassinations – whatever they had to do to achieve their goals was done. The Black Nobility was obsessed with being on top and left nothing to chance. Morality was for the little people.

As Ivan Cloulas wrote in *The Borgias,* "Starting from the late 11th century, the dependency of the Byzantine Empire on the navies of the Republic of Venice and, to a lesser extent, the Republic of Genoa and the Republic of Pisa, led to the predominance of Catholic merchants in Byzantium, which had received major trading concessions since the 1080s, subsequently causing economic and social upheaval. Together with the perceived arrogance of the Italians, it fueled popular resentment amongst the middle and lower classes both in the countryside and in the cities. (By) the second half of the 12th century, the practically uncontrollable rivalry among competitors from the different city-states devolved to the point that Italians were raiding the quarters of other Italians in the capital, and retaliatory draconian measures by the Byzantine authorities led to the deterioration of inter-religious relations in the city. Byzantine foreign policy was invariably perceived as sinister and anti-Latin in the West."

With powerful merchants seeking new markets, the Vatican looked towards acquiring land in North America, the home to an estimated 100,000 to 300,000 indigenous people who had migrated from Asia over a land bridge called Beringia during the Ice Age. Before the Papacy could claim the land for the Catholic Church, the Vatican needed to ensure that no rival power could claim it first.

Norse explorers from Greenland were the first Europeans to arrive in North America between the 10th and 15th centuries. The Norse presence in North American was confirmed with the discovery of L'Anse aux Meadows in 1906 on the northwestern most tip of the Great Northern Peninsula on the island of Newfoundland in the Canadian province of Newfoundland and Labrador.

Why did it take so long to make this discovery? The Norse explorers disappeared without a trace after having succumbed to some type of extermination event. Some historians blamed the Black Death, which killed between 75 and 200 million people in Eurasia after traders brought the disease back from the Orient. Others believed the Norse were massacred by the Indians whom they had befriended.

What is known is that at the time of their disappearance, the Scandinavia Vikings and Norse were establishing themselves as maritime traders in Northern Europe and forging markets throughout the British Isles, Western Europe, and Asia. Extermination was a military tactic employed by Central Asian warlords – and subsequently picked up by Western merchants who traded with them. If one tribe or clan of merchants wanted land or resources claimed by another, the former would stage an extermination event, eliminate the human obstacles, and then seize whatever it wanted.

The disappearance of the Norse colonies coincided with the rise of the Hanseatic League in the Frankish Holy Roman Empire (HRE) which had forged an alliance with the Vatican. The HRE's kontors (trading posts) reached into London, Flanders, and Norway, linking guilds that provided mutual benefit for participating traders. For example, League members enjoyed protections from piracy, access to coveted markets, tax and trade concessions, and extraterritoriality agreements that allowed traders to do business overseas under the laws of the League.

The Hanseatic League became the driving economic force behind prosperity in Northern European, bringing enormous wealth to its participants. Moreover, it was modeled after the guilds of Central Asia, which facilitated trade and promoted surveillance to preempt attacks, protect markets, and intercept communications from rivals.

Most people who praise the Hanseatic League cannot see past its enormous profits and therefore promote the guild model as a basis for regional and global markets. Profit seeking without an ethical base or structure leads to plunder, piracy, and an incestuous relationship between governments and big business that rots society and industry from within. The League was conductive to market rigging, squashing independent businesses, and monopolies. As long as money was being made, participating merchants never questioned its tactics. Yet, what the Hanseatic League established was a criminal enterprise backed by the Vatican and governments who served a parasitical elite at the expense of the people and the countries in which they operated, with the governments providing the weapons and military to defend and expand their markets throughout the world.

At its peak, the Hanseatic League spanned across 170

communities, enabling Hanseatic merchants to import grains, wax, fish, metal ores, and other raw materials in exchange for textiles and apparel.

The key export that enabled them to acquire wealth was silk, a product made cheaply in Central Asia which was in high demand among Europeans. Acquiring access to silk and the secrets to creating it were jealously guarded; the Central Asians weren't about to part with them without demanding concessions in return. Thus began the infiltration of Asian values into the West.

While lacking a permanent administrative body, treasury, and standing military, the Hanseatic League forged powerful alliances with mercenaries based upon kinship. With increasing frequency, powerful League members were able to stage blockades and declare war. Given its effectiveness, the League became the template for Rothschild's European Coal and Steel Community, a precursor to the European Union, which became the model for regional free markets around the world.

In 1494, Russian Tsar Ivan III, who had effectively repelled Central Asian invasions into Russia, closed the Hanseatic Kontor in Novgorod over its unscrupulous practices. An uncompromising defender of the Christian faith, Ivan the Great aspired to establish a Third Rome, with the first being Rome and the second being Constantinople. As secularism spread throughout Eurasia, Russia defended Christianity from foreign assaults.

In 1597, Queen Elizabeth I expelled League members from London and sponsored Sir Walter Raleigh and Sir Francis Bacon's journey to North America to create colonies of, by, and for a free people under God for Great Britain. The Merchants of London were eager to forge new markets but wanted to pursue new lines of trade in a benevolent fashion based upon ethics and Biblical principles and so the Queen chartered the East India Company (EIC) for this purpose.

No one ever discovered what happened to the Norse – but their fate mirrors that of other merchants who encroached into the markets coveted by Catholic Monarchs, the Vatican, and their affiliated merchant families.

Mongolian Hordes

The Mongols had been invading Europe for centuries. By the 13th century, Christian missionaries ventured into Central Asia to convert the barbarian hordes to Christianity in a vain attempt to civilize them, conscript them into the service of the Catholic Church, and collect information on them for the purposes of facilitating commerce.

Jesuit and Franciscan missionaries were among the first to venture into Central Asia on behalf of the Catholic Church. While the Jesuits were profit-motivated and schooled in subversive tactics, the Franciscans were somewhat more sincere in their efforts, as demonstrated by their willingness to take a poverty oath.

The Franciscan Order was founded by St. Francis of Assisi. Pope Innocent III agreed to approve the order as long as the Franciscans emulated the life of Jesus by reducing themselves to begging while preaching the Gospel so that they would be forced to rely upon God and the good will of others for their survival. Perhaps they were reduced to this state so as not to pose a threat to the more powerful Jesuits.

As usual, the Catholic Church misrepresented Jesus in order to discount his power. While the Jesuses believed their treasures were in heaven, both Jesuses were prosperous, with one establishing Britain's banking system and the other excelling in architecture. They did not beg or expect others to subsidize their ministry. Rather, they advocated compassion for the less fortunate, to give and help as God directed.

If the Vatican were sincere in its effort to gain converts, it might have chosen to support the Franciscans financially. The Vatican was flush with cash, but as the Pope appreciated, the poor Franciscans provided good public relations for the church, which begged for donations to help the poor while its leaders became exceedingly rich.

To their credit, the Franciscans devoted themselves to a life in service of God. Given their good intentions, they were able to establish amicable relations with the Mongolians, who had established one of the largest empires in Central Asia. As meticulous record keepers, the Franciscans documented what they observed of Mongolian empire. They mapped out the topography and architecture and recorded Mongolian customs, religion, and commercial strategies. All findings were reported and archived at the Vatican.

Yet this was not a benevolent Christian land. The ancient Greeks characterized Tartaros (Tartary) as a prison for the mythological Gods. Written in the eighth century BC, Homer's *Iliad* depicted Zeus threatening to throw the disobedient "down to the murk of Tartaros, far below, where the uttermost depth of the pit lies under Earth, where there are gates of iron and a brazen door stone, as far beneath the house of Hades, as from Earth the sky lies."

Ancient writers portrayed Tartaros as "the dungeon of the damned" and a "chamber of torments" that was located in "the deepest recesses of the flat Earth as the sky rose about the Earth."

According to one myth, the goddess Gaia mated with a "primordial deity of the Tartarean pit" and spawned "a monstrous serpentine storm-giant," which Zeus squashed and threw into the pits of Tartaros.

Fairy Tail Wiki Fandom describes Tartaros as "one of the most powerful Dark Guilds in the world – (one) comprised mostly of (demons) and the strongest, most evil Mage of all time."

These descriptions mirrored the strange depictions of creatures and evil recorded in Marco Polo's adventures into Central Asia and in the meticulously kept records of Catholic missionaries and explorers who entered these dark lands. The 17th century Anglo-Irish author Jonathan Swift depicted giants, Lilliputians, and other curious people in his acclaimed novel, *Gulliver's Travelers,* in which he satirically portrays different tribes the explorers and merchants encountered during their journeys. Before these people were erased from history, British novelists immortalized them in novels.

Giants and other mythological people were reputedly scattered throughout the disparate tribes of Central Asia only to be wiped out through one extermination event after another. The elites didn't want the public to know what had happened to them or why. With awareness of the agenda and strategies in play, the people might be empowered to overthrow their tyrants and remove the shackles that bound them.

As the Vatican strengthened diplomatic relations with the Mongolian rulers, representatives of the Catholic Church spread, secularism, paganism, and the rational Enlightenment throughout Europe, planting the seeds that would ultimately lead to Europe's decline. One Franciscan missionary, Giovanni da Montecorvino (1246-

1328), was appointed archbishop of Peking and Roman legate to the Mongolian Great Khan. Another Franciscan missionary, Odorico da Pordenone (1265-1331), facilitated communications between the Vatican and Mongols in Russia. In 1254, an Italian explorer by the name of Giovanni da Pian del Carpine, journeyed into Tartaros, where he met the Great Khan of the Mongolian Empire.

The Pope directed his missionaries to see if they could convert the Mongolians to Catholicism, but conversion proved to be an exercise in futility. As the Khan advised, the Mongols had conquered Central Asia and were destined to rule the world. At the same time, he agreed to allow Christians to enter his kingdom. As the Great Khan said: "There are four great Prophets who are revered and worshiped by the different classes of mankind. The Christians regard Jesus Christ as their divinity; the Saracens, Mahomet; the Jews, Moses, and the idolaters, Sogomombar-kan, the most eminent amongst their idols. I do honor and show respect to all the four and invoke to my aid whichever amongst them is in truth Supreme in Heaven."

Why not convert to Christianity then, the missionaries asked.

"Wherefore should I become a Christian – you yourselves must perceive that the Christians of these countries are ignorant, inefficient persons, who do not possess the faculty of performing anything miraculous, whereas you see that the idolaters can do whatever they will," the Great Khan replied.

As the missionaries listened on, the Khan clarified:

When I sit, the cups that were in the middle of the hall come to me filled with wine and other beverages, spontaneously and without being touched by human hands, and I drink from them.

(We) have the power of controlling the weather and obliging it to retire to any quarter of the heavens with many other wonderful gifts of that nature.

You are witness that idols have the faculty of speed and predict whatever is required.

Should I become a convert to the faith of Christ and profess myself a Christian, the nobles of my court and other persons who do not incline to that religion will ask me what sufficient motives have caused me to receive baptism and embrace Christianity. What extraordinary powers, they will say, what miracles have been displayed by its ministers? Whereas the idolaters declared that what they exhibit is performed through their own sanctity and the influence of their idols.

To this, I shall not know what answers to make, and I shall be considered by them as laboring under an error whilst the idolaters who, by means of their profound art, can effect such wonders may without difficulty compass my death.

The Khan then told the disappointed missionaries that if they could prove they had superior powers through Jesus Christ, he might consider converting:

Return you to your pontiff and request of him, in my name, to send hither a hundred persons well skilled in your law who being confronted with the idolaters shall have power to restrain them and showing that they themselves are endowed with similar art but which they refrain from exercising because it is derived from the agency of evil spirits, shall compel them to desist from practices of such a nature in their presence.

When I am witness of this, I shall place them and their religion under a ban and shall allow myself to be baptized.

Following my example, all my nobility will then in like manner receive baptism, and this will be imitated by my subjects in general.

In the end, the Christians of these parts will exceed in number those who inhabit your own country.

The missionaries immediately reported the good news to the Pope who eagerly dispatched missionaries to Mongolia to teach the Gospel.

Neither the Great Khan nor his subjects proved to be eager students. Rather, the students ended up teaching the teachers. As leading British socialist philosopher Bertrand Russell wrote in *The Problem with China*: "When I went to China, I went to teach, but every day I stayed, I thought less of what I had to teach and more of what I had to learn."

At the same time, the merchants recorded that in Sin-Gui, the Mongols/Tartars possessed "vast quantities of raw silk and manufacturing for their own consumption. There are among them some very rich merchants, and the number of the inhabitants is so great as to be the subject of astonishment. They are a cowardly race and solely occupied with their trade and manufacturing. They display considerable ability, and if they were as enterprising, manly, and warlike as they are ingenious, so vast is their number that they might not only subdue the whole of the province, but might carry their views still further."

Described as a "silk center (whose) weavers are divided up into powerful guilds called the Nankin and Suchau," the Sin-Gui fanned across 16 wealthy cities and towns where trade flourished.

The guilds in the "City of Earth" made their fortunes manufacturing silk and marketing their products through alliances forged in Europe and Central Asia. Missionaries reported that they passed through "many towns, castles, and villages, all of them well inhabited and opulent. The people have abundance of provision."

The Vatican and its merchants salivated over the profits that stood to be made and so decided to subdue this area so they could corner the markets before rival European interests had the chance.

While exploring Mongolia, the missionaries stumbled upon Kin-Sai, otherwise known as the Celestial City. As the missionaries observed, Kin-Sai was overflowing with decadence which eventually spilled over into Judeo-Christian countries by way of commerce. The unrestrained sensuality and debauchery they discovered helped spawn a culture of libertinism throughout the West. Since the merchants revered the wealthy Central Asians, they held their values and practices as superior to their own and eventually adopted and promoted them. As the missionaries described Kin-Sai:

In the streets are the quarters of the courtesans who are here in such numbers as I dare not venture to report. Not only near the squares which is the situation usually appropriated for their residence, but in every part of the city, they are to be found, adorned much in finery, highly perfumed, occupying well furnished houses and attended by many female domestics.

These women are accomplished and are perfect in the arts of caressing and fondling, which they accompany with expressions adapted to every description of person.

Strangers who have once tasted of their charms remain in a state of fascination and become so enhanced by their own wanton arts, that they can never forget the impression.

Thus intoxicated with sensual pleasures, when they return to their homes, they report that they have been in Kin-Sai, or the Celestial City, and look forward to the time when they may be enabled to revisit to this paradise.

In other streets are the dwellings of the physicians and the astrologers who also give instructions in reading and writing.

At the end of three days, you reach the noble and magnificent city of Kin-Sai, a name that signifies The Celestial City, and which it merits from its preeminence to all others in the world in point of grandeur and beauty as well as from its abundance delights, which might lead an inhabitant to imagine himself in paradise."

Throughout their journey into Central Asia, the explorers and missionaries encountered "magicians, enchanters, and astrologers." The tribes were not all Asian either. Some they encountered were described as "men and women (with) fair complexion (who) are handsome."

The Central Asian culture and traditions soon spread throughout Europe. While Christians rejected psychics and astrologers, one missionary wrote:

In the City of Kin-Sai, they inquire of an astrologer under what sign or aspect of the heavens the child was born, and his answer is likewise committed carefully to writing.

When, therefore, he is grown up and is about to engage in any mercantile adventure, voyage, or treaty of marriage, this document is carried to the astrologer, who having examined it and weighed all the circumstances, pronounces certain oracular words in which these people who sometimes find themselves justified by the events, place great confidence.

Of these astrologers, or rather magicians, great numbers are to be met with in every marketplace, and no marriage is ever celebrated until an opinion has been pronounced upon it by one of that profession.

While Christians had rejected soothsayers and astrologers, the

East had opened the door to new religions, leading to a decline in the church and growing interest in the occult. Astrological forecasts now appear in mainstream newspapers and popular selling books while psychics are enlisted to advise celebrities among others seeking answers through the occult. Even President Reagan's wife, Nancy, famously consulted astrologers before making important decisions.

While Westerners paid taxes for the purposes of supporting basic government functions, the merchants observed that additional "wealth (could be) generated by paying tax to the King." The taxes weren't used for any reason beyond feeding the coffers of the rich and making the rich even richer off the backs of the poor through the strong arm of a tyrannical government. Since the rich and powerful were considered to hold a mandate from Heaven, they felt entitled to exploit the poor in this fashion, concluding that the misery of the afflicted was a consequence of God's abandonment of them. These self-serving attitudes eventually found their way into the West in the form of objectivism and the "prosperity Gospel."

The missionaries also observed that the Mongolians cataloged and tracked each subject from birth and then generated profits throughout their lives, a practice the Vatican adopted and which formed the basis of Prince Philip and the Rothschild's *Silent Weapons for Quiet Wars* – a plan to catalog, track, and trace each person on Earth through a technocracy which sought to maximize a person's output while rationing what he could receive in return to that which was sufficient for basic survival and procreation. As the emissaries observed in Central Asia: "Leaders keep tabs on every citizen, who lives, who dies. They catalog people. Births are registered, and citizens under the dominion of the Great Khan are kept dependent."

The Vatican learned that its own power could be enhanced by reducing people to dependency and abject poverty. This outcome could be accomplished by redistributing wealth upwards and demoralizing people beneath them, forcing the people to rely upon the government and the church, rather than themselves, for survival. In the process, the government, and ultimately, the Vatican, would be elevated to the status of God on Earth.

The Mongolian elite revered the Buddhist lamas who engaged in terrifying occult rituals that facilitated the transmigration of souls from one person to the next, from human to animal, and from the dead to the living. They also practiced what was described as a form of Tengrism, or ancestor worship, involving shamanism, animism, totemism, and demon possession.

Through the deft use of the occult, black magic, barbarism, oppressive control mechanisms, and war, the Mongols established a vast empire called Pax Mongolia, which lasted about a century (1260-1368) and extended throughout Central Asia, parts of India, Turkey, and even into the Arctic.

The Mongolians also established trading posts to disseminate mail, like the Pony Express. These posts enabled merchants and rulers to communicate with each other, intercept each others mail, and facilitate commerce, forming what eventually became the basis for the Office of Strategic Services, MI5, MI6, Mossad, CIA, and other intelligence services, which eventually formed the Five Eyes. The purpose of surveillance wasn't to protect nations, but to surveil the public, leaders, and rival businesses on behalf of private corporations whose interests often did not coincide with the national or public interest.

The missionaries were quick to notice that the Khans preferred to have slaves wait on them hand and foot. When not otherwise slashing and burning their way through Central Asia, the Mongols were an indolent people who were "little disposed to any toil, even to that of the chase," one missionary observed. "They neither sow nor reap, nor plow or burrow." Rather, they wiled away their hours drinking themselves into oblivion, scheming, and afflicting suffering upon others.

While the Vatican plotted the conquest of the Mongols, the missionaries diligently mapped out the topography of Central Asia, documenting each mountain, stream, and valley, notating the architectural structures and the lay of the land, ensuring that when time arrived for the Vatican to pull the trigger, the lazy Mongols would be caught off guard. What the Jesuits lacked in swashbuckling brutality, they made up for in ingenuity; Jesuit plots were ruthlessly executed with precision, leaving nothing to chance.

There was no point in trying to convert the Mongolian or their slaves to Catholicism, the missionaries concluded, as they go "where they are led, not where they choose to go."

Despite their patient dedication to imparting the Gospel on the hordes, the Mongols refused to listen or learn anything new. The Jesuits absolutely "abhorred (the Mongols) in their hearts as men unclean and destitute of arts and sciences." Missionaries described their priests and lamas as "very ignorant (and prone) to debauchery, especially with the women whom they abuse with impunity."

By the 14th century, the Franciscans had established academic societies in Jerusalem and Hong Kong while the Vatican set the stage for the conquest of Central Asia. One Franciscan, Giovanni di Monte Corvina, taught the *Bible* in Beijing. While the missionaries maintained a clean Christian image, the Vatican became "a violent, blood-red world, a world of luxury, sensuality, and death, where poison and the dagger rule," Ivan Cloulas wrote in *The Borgias*. "Arrayed in the silks and gold, incest and murder, the forces of evil dragged the head of God's Church to the very abyss of hell."

While Jesuits wielded daggers behind their backs, the arrogant Mongols remained oblivious and convinced of their own invincibility. Then, like a bolt out of the blue, revolution broke out, and just like that, one of the most powerful dynasties in world was conquered.

The leader of the revolution was a Buddhist missionary by the name of Zhu Yuanzhang (Taizu), who "liberated" China from the Mongols. Supporting him were "men of force" who executed a well-coordinated coup.

During this revolution, as was typical of the revolutions that would later burn through Europe, Mongolian treasures were looted and hauled away. The thieves knew exactly what they were looking for. They knew what to take and how to locate the loot, as if the plunder had been meticulously planned well in advance.

The Jesuits were among the first to greet and congratulate Taizu, who established the Ming dynasty (1368-1644). The new Central Asian leadership proved much more open to diplomacy with the Vatican. For the first time, the Jesuits were allowed to establish an apostolate (office or mission of an apostle) in Macao and Canton.

The so-called people's revolution was organized by the "White Lotus Society," otherwise known as the "Chinese Freemasons." Just like its Western counterparts, this secret society required blood oaths and engaged in subversive activities against governments.

The Jesuits had been observing the Buddhist monastery when they noticed that the men serving under the lamas were being sodomized. Somehow they decided that Taizu was sufficiently browbeaten and complaint to be their man.

While enjoying the trust of their Mongolian hosts, the Jesuits recruited Taizu into the White Lotus Society. An obscure man from a humble background, Taizu rose through the ranks, with the help of the Jesuits, to lead a revolution starting with the successful invasion of Nanjing. From there, the rebels struck out at regional warlords, whose whereabouts and particulars had been mapped out well in advance.

In 1368, as the weakest links of the empire fell, Taizu was directed to overthrow the Mongolian rulers by storming their Beijing palaces, forcing them to flee with their tails between their legs. Once the Mongols capitulated, the Ming dynasty was established.

Taizu followed a pattern typical of communist rulers. Upon assuming power, he set up a secret police force that identified and squashed conspiracies hatched by rivals and executed 100,000 enemies of the state.

The secret society that had orchestrated his rise to power was so-named White Lotus to represent the traitor behind the mask of virtue – a name befitting the Jesuits. As a flower that rises above the mud to reach the sun, the lotus represents the process of purifying the darkness of ignorance to reach enlightenment. This perspective was Buddhist to the core and consistent with the principles of the rational Enlightenment which would later spur revolution throughout Eurasia and North America, toppling governments, starting with the European Monarchs who held the "divine right (rite) to rule."

The Jesuits in Central Asia were impressed with the revolutionary aspects of Confucianism – that of mobilizing the poor to overthrow the rich in order to establish a new order for the wannabe rich. The poor were just a means to an end. After the rich and powerful were overthrown, executed, and separated from their wealth, a new ruling class would emerge.

In *Religion in Chinese Society*, C.K Yang wrote: "From the earliest times, religion has universally performed the unique function of producing a picture of life different from that in concrete existence and hence the morally uplifting effect of religion in changing the world to conform to the imaginary or ideal pattern as conceived by the founders. Religion has always sought to differ from and not to conform to reality in contrast to the traditional reality-bound Confucian orthodoxy. Religion contains a seed of revolution except when it is thoroughly diffused or merged into the established moral and political institutions as the Chinese classical religion was."

Reflecting the hidden hand in play, the capital of the Ming dynasty (1368-1644) was established in Beijing. Its seat of government was held in the Forbidden City, which was fortified against military invasions just as the Vatican had been.

Only the "rulers of the realm" were allowed entry. Government functionaries and the imperial family were refused access, not unlike agencies in the United States federal government where members of the Senior Executive Service and intelligence communities have access to intelligence, resources, and power that are beyond the reach of the President.

The fingerprints of the Vatican were there as evidenced in the Ming dynasty's decision to name the Forbidden City's entrance the Meridian Gate in recognition of Jesus who established the Meridian Time Zone. Since Chinese Emperors believed themselves to be the "Sons of Heaven" who lived at "the center of the universe," the Society of Jesus placed that center at the Meridian Gate while claiming the Vatican held God's temporal authority on Earth through St. Peter.

The five doors to the Meridian Gate were arranged to reaffirm the power and status of the Emperor who exclusively held the right to enter the middle passageway. Bells were rung to announce his trip to the Temple of Heaven while drums signaled his journey to the Ancestral Temple.

Taizu was succeeded by his son, Chengzu, who expanded the Chinese tribute system to India, the Persian Gulf, and the eastern part of Africa. As Emperor, Chengzu demanded that these countries submit to China's demands and place its interests first. All nations were to prostrate themselves before the new Chinese ruler, who was secretly managed by the Jesuits.

By submitting to China, they were submitting to the Vatican. At the same time, the Pope virtue signaled from the pulpit and demanded that countries embrace values and submit to policies in the name of Jesus that advanced the interests of powerful merchant classes with stakes in the lucrative markets of Central Asia.

Alfonso de Borgia (Pope Callixtus III) presided over the Papacy from 1455 to 1458. As a cleric born in Kingdom of Valencia, he gathered his family around the throne of St. Peter to establish a dynasty of priests whose influence had spread throughout Italy, Rome, France, and Spain.

The bull on the de Borgia coat-of-arms was set to a red background to represent the family's pastoral origins and the fierce warrior spirit of this clan. The de Borgia dynasty owes its Royal heritage to Spanish King Jaime who bequeathed some of his land to Esteban de Borgia.

In the 14th century, one branch of the de Borgia family migrated to Naples, Italy while the rest remained in Spain. Kinship ties were maintained through matrimonial lines, ensuring an enduring alliance between the Vatican and the Spanish Monarchy.

As a result of the Great Schism of 1378, factions from Rome and Avignon contested the Papacy. Alfonso then became the compromise candidate.

Alfonso served as a cardinal and representative at the Holy Sea who answered to the King of Naples as the Orsinis and Colonnas battled for control of Rome. As one Cardinal wrote of the Vatican: "Here knowledge and merit count for nothing." His advice to the virtuous who aspired to a career in the Catholic Church was: "don't lose heart. Spend some time unlearning what you know and learning the vices you don't know if you wish to get in the Pope's good graces." The vow of celibacy was flouted every day, and pedophilia, which Plato had characterized as the practice of manly men, was rampant among priests.

In 1454, the Holy See formed a League to ensure "peace and repose in Italy in defense of the Christian faith" for 25 years. Through the authority vested in the Vatican, the Pope appointed cardinals based upon nepotism or bribery. Most were drawn from prominent Italian and Spanish families, with few recruited from Germany or France. "An extremely elaborate tax system made it possible to line the papal coffers and at the same time dole out handsome sums to the chancellor staff," Cloulas wrote.

While claiming to be a staunch defender of Christianity, the Pope routinely betrayed the faith. In one instance, the Pope's loyalties were called into question after the Ottoman Empire's Sultan Bayezid II gifted him the holy spear Roman soldier Longinus used to pierce Jesus on the cross.

At the same, pagan symbols began appearing throughout the Vatican and its territories. While the Pope claimed divine authority from Jesus by way of St. Peter, a statue of the Greek god Apollo was discovered at Porto d'Anzo. "In the Rome of the Popes so easily excited over ancient pagan remains, no one was shocked by anything, be it priestly immorality or scandals in the Curia," Cloulas wrote. "One night the pontifical police arrested six people for producing and selling forged bulls. The seller, Francesco Maldente, was a canon of Forli, the forger, Dominico Gentile di Viterbo, a papal scrivener and son of one of the Pope's doctors."

Sexual immorality was rampant at the Vatican. The problem of prostitution reportedly got so bad that in 1490 that one of the papal vicars felt compelled to tell priests and laymen living in Rome to "get rid of their public or secret concubines" or face excommunication. As far as the Vatican was concerned, "respectable courtesans added to the magnificence of the cardinals courts, where they held salons and enhanced the splendor of the ceremonies with their sumptuous gowns and jewels" Cloulas wrote.

The Vatican and its staff presented themselves as Royalty and spent money like drunken sailors. According to one historian: "The cardinals appeared in public, on foot or on horseback, with a costly sword at their side. Each one had a staff of several hundred servants in his palace who summoned at will those mercenaries known as bravi. Furthermore, they had a circle of dependents, men of the people, whom they entertained at their expense. Almost all had their particular faction, and they vied with each other in pomp, especially at times of cavalcades or carnivals when channels bearing masked men, troupes of singers, or players costumed at their expense rode through the city. The cardinals outdid the old Roman barons."

By the 15th century, Church corruption was so pronounced that believers feared God's retribution was close at hand. While Popes promised to give to the poor, the poor they had in mind were themselves. The Vatican promised material rewards for toadies who served the papal hierarchy, a practice now commonplace among the American federal government, which has transformed into a moral cesspool in the mold of the Vatican.

Consolidating Power

While the Vatican was consolidating its power in China, explorers for Catholic Monarchs were seeking to claim North America for the Catholic Church.

Rodrigo de Borgia became Pope Alexander VI in 1492 around the time Christopher Columbus set sail for the West Indies on behalf of the Spanish Monarchy. The following year, Columbus returned to Spain to report that he had found a possible western route to China in the new world.

On May 4, 1443, Pope Alexander VI attempted to make the discovery official through a bull that delineated the boundaries of the Spanish and Portuguese empires as both rivaled each other for a western route to the Indies. "In these unknown lands where Christopher Columbus has stepped, (there are) naked vegetarians who believe in one God and ask to be taught to believe in Jesus Christ," Pope Alexander VI wrote. "All these lands and territories abounding in gold, spices, and treasure situated west and south of a line that runs from the North and South are allocated to the Catholic Kings on condition that they are not discovered before the preceding Christmas by another Christian prince. This act is established by virtue of the authority of the Almighty God bestowed on the blessed Peter and the right of the Vicarite of Jesus Christ which the pontiff exercises upon Earth."

In other words, the Pope claimed North America for the Catholic Church. If another ruler entered the demarcated area for trade or other purposes without the permission of the Vatican, he would be excommunicated. Since the Vatican lacked official authority, beyond that which it had claimed for itself, the Pope arguably had no authority to make its land claims binding.

Once the English began to colonize North American in the 17th century, the Jesuits mobilized the Indians to attack them to prevent the colonists from expanding westward into what they considered to be Vatican territory. Revolution followed soon after under the rallying cry of "no taxation without representation," a common refrain in Jesuit/Marxist-inspired revolutions.

Before the War for Independence, the colonists and British Monarch were on amicable terms and had open lines of communications through diplomatic channels in which disputes and grievances were resolved. As reported in *Royal Blood Lies,* the grievances between both parties were spurred by agitators who sought to separate Great Britain from its colonies and place both in debt and under the control of international bankers and foreign interests. "Thanks to the Borgia Pope, (Spanish King) Ferdinand and (Queen) Isabella now had their right to the Americas," Cloulas wrote. "The Spaniards had the best possible insurance for the future of their conquests."

Upon securing the Papacy, Rodrigo de Borgia (Pope Alexander VI) set out to consolidate his power by making his allies cardinals. He also attempted to represent that he held the divine right to rule by enlisting a painter from the Sistine Chapel to design illustrations in allegorical style that reflected his aspirations.

The Pope's apartment was graced with scenes from the *New Testament* which represented the mysteries of the Christian faith, including the Annunciation, Nativity, Epiphany, Resurrection, Assumption, and Pentecost. "In the scene of the resurrection," Cloulas wrote, "Alexander is seen kneeling before Christ's tomb from which the Savior ascends into heaven." The Pope was depicted wearing his ceremonial, jewel-studded robe with a golden tiara placed beside him so that others would believe he had "received the blessing of the resurrected Christ."

In Central Asia, magic and power were conveyed through art, the Vatican learned. Through these depictions then, de Borgia sought to assert papal supremacy as part of a power move to establish "a bond between himself and the living God (so that) he alone had the right to transmit God's will to mankind," Cloulas wrote.

At the same time, the ceilings of de Borgia's apartment were replete with images of the pagan gods, Isis and Osiris, revealing his "fondness for the esoteric" along with his "dynasty pride." Since Osiris was transformed into the sacred bull, Apis, after his death, and the bull was represented on the family crest, de Borgia attempted to establish the "totemic link between the Pope and Egyptian God."

At the Pope's request, a commentary was written under the frescoes to clarify the message de Borgia wanted to convey through these images: "By escaping the wiles of the devil, (man) could, like Osiris, be reborn for eternity."

In the wake of external threats from infidels, French, English, Austrian, and Spanish Monarchs buried the hatchet and forged alliances with each other for mutual protection, not fully understanding the extent to which the Vatican was bankrolling the attacks against them. The Vatican enjoyed an amicable relationship with the Turkish empire through the Jesuits, Greeks, and merchants who did business in Central Asia, and so infidel mercenaries could be called upon to do the Pope's bidding.

Rather than use its diplomatic position to forge peace in the region, the Pope fomented war to secure financial gain and territory for the Vatican. In an effort to protect Christendom, French King Charles VIII led a crusade against the Turkish claim to the throne of Naples, which had been linked to the throne of Jerusalem since the 13th century. The Pope responded by backing Naples.

"Charles VIII announced that the object of his expedition to Naples was to prepare for the destruction of Turkish power and liberation of the Holy Land and demanded that the Pope grant him free passage through the papal territories," Cloulas wrote. "The Pope was embarrassed as his papal envoy, Giorgio Buzardo, had been captured at Sinigaglia on the Adriatic coast (and) was on his way back from Istanbul, bearing letters from the (Turkish) Bayezid II assuring Rome of his support against the French. The revelation of an alliance between the Vicar of Christ and that of Mahomet created an enormous scandal."

After Columbus died in 1506, the Americas were named Amerigo Vespucci to recognize the continent as a unique land mass. Other Castellians traveled across the Pacific to Southeast Asia. The Spanish Monarch, which was working hand-in-glove with the Vatican, then set out to claim North America for the Catholic Church. In 1562, Juan Rodriguez Cabriallo's expedition to California incorporated the state into "New Spain."

Catholic missions sprouted up throughout California as military and trading posts similar to those erected throughout Central Asia by the Mongols and Italian merchants.

At the same time, Jesuit missionaries, like Martino Martini (1614-1661), were making inroads into China. In 1651, Martini returned to Europe as Procurator of the China mission with detailed maps of all the Chinese provinces along with observations and research on the Ming dynasty. His work contained the coordinates of Chinese cities, including longitudes and latitudes, the names of the mountains, rivers, and people, with annotations of distances, transcriptions, and pronunciation of Chinese characters. While his work was historical and factual in nature, it was particularly useful to the Vatican for the purposes of intelligence gathering and conquest. Divide-and-conquer tactics were employed in areas the Vatican sought to rule.

In the Spanish colonies in America and elsewhere, reports began circulating that the merchants were harming the indigenous people. In 1511, a friar named Antonio de Montesino asked the Spanish by what right they had invaded, enslaved, raped, tortured, and robbed people who had done them no harm. A Dominican priest by the name of Bartoleme de La Casas posed similar questions over the needless deaths of indigenous peoples who were Spanish subjects.

King Charles VIII responded by imposing new laws prohibiting owners of encomiendas from enslaving or harming the Indians. The indigenous people, he said, were a free people with rights under God. The conquistadors were furious over the new laws and rebelled, putting further strain between the Spanish Monarchy and its colonies, which were suddenly seeking independence.

What the Spanish Monarchs failed to appreciate is that commercial relations with China had placed its overseas merchants at an unfair advantage. The merchants were falling into debt and desperately needed silver to rectify trade imbalances with China. With limited labor and resources at hand and demands for payment increasing, the conquistadors exploited the cheap labor available.

There were reports that the Jesuits and missionaries were aware of the commercial strains placed on Catholic merchants in North America, but chose to exacerbate friction between the Spanish Monarchy and its colonies to separate them so that land holdings and resources could be consolidated into fewer hands with the goal of having the Vatican control all territory in the world.

The missionaries and Jesuits certainly turned a blind eye to the slaughter of tribal peoples in Central Asia in their quest to consolidate power for the Vatican. That they were concerned enough over Indians performing cheap labor in North America to enlist the Spanish Monarchs to intervene reflects that a different agenda was at play.

King Charles I of Spain, like Ferdinand and Isabela before him and Philip II after him, demanded that indigenous people of North America be paid a fair wage for their work at a time when the merchants were struggling to pay their bills.

By the 17th century, the Italian merchants saw their maritime empires crumble. The power dynamics had changed. At the same time, Great Britain was rising as a maritime power. Queen Elizabeth I had just chartered the East India Company (EIC) to establish new markets in North America and around the world for the British Empire. With their knowledge of new trade routes and alliances with mercenary forces from Central Asia, the Italian merchants were able to infiltrate the EIC during the reign of King James I, transforming the East India Company into a force for imperialism and conquest.

In light of the Vatican's relentless assaults on Christian countries, Anglo-Irish author Jonathan Swift wrote *An Argument Against Abolishing Christianity* to defend the faith. He further confronted the degeneracy and evil creeping into Britain by way of a predatory merchant class by suggesting, in his satirical *Modest Proposal,* that the poor Irish might consider selling their children to wealthy cannibals to pay their bills.

In 1620, as the Pilgrims set sail for America, the EIC was making inroads into Africa and Asia. Two years later, White Lotus rebels were once again fomenting regime change in Central Asia. In 1644, the Ming dynasty fell. The next dynasty would be even more accommodating to the Vatican.

Confucius Says

Christian missionaries returning from China raised the question of whether the Catholic Church should be supporting Confucius leaders who worshiped their ancestors and engaged in occult rituals. After all, such practices had been forbidden in the *Bible* and were incompatible with Christianity.

The Jesuits, who had already embraced the power of the occult, didn't take issue with Confucianism, which also provided the rationale for usury as a means to impose power over others through financial control and debt. Italian merchants were facing interest rates for loans far in excess of the going interest rate based upon the high risk of doing business in Central Asia, but the risk was being created and managed by mercenaries who ultimately answered to Jesuit-controlled Asian rulers and the Vatican. Had they known the source of the financial controls, these merchants could have appealed to their allies at the Vatican for more favorable lending conditions. Concerned over the extent to which Confucianism was corrupting Christian society, Dominican and Franciscan missionaries requested that the Vatican render a judgment on the Chinese Rites controversy.

The controversy began in 1645 after the Dominicans submitted a brief, entitled *The Congregation of the Propagation of the Faith,* to compel the Vatican to reject Confucianism. Given the influence of the Vatican over local parishes, Jesuits were able to convince Christian ministers to lift the ban, reflecting the degree to which Christian churches and their leaders were compromised. Confucianism was being "perfected" by Christianity, they maintained as they tried to draw parallels between the two. Somehow the Dominicans and Franciscans came to share the Jesuits' tolerance for Confucianism. Lest anyone question the extent to which the Vatican was betraying Christianity, Pope Clement XI banned the rites in 1704, and four decades later, Pope Benedict XIV reaffirmed the prohibitions.

Buried within Confucianism were the seeds of communism, globalism, and revolution that were driving progress towards a modernity that was consolidating the world's wealth and power into the hands of a few. Confucianism held that the rites were intentional and significant acts of social unification that established a social hierarchy and maintained control. Within this hierarchy, everyone was to know his place. "Let rulers be rulers and ministers be ministers," Confucius said. (*The Analects 12:11*)

Through the principle of "rectifying names," the elite were to redistribute wealth from the people to themselves, reside in palatial mansions, and wear the most expensive finery while the slaves were relegated to languishing in slums, being financially exploited, and wearing rags. California's tent cities, where the homeless congregate, are a reflection of a broken system and failed government that has betrayed its people, but to the followers of Confucianism, the losers in globalism should be confined to living in cardboard boxes as is befitting their status as the newly subjugated class while the elite fly overhead in private jets, with no demonstrable concern displayed for the plight of the poor.

Karl Marx, the author of the *Communist Manifesto*, once remarked that "revolutions are the locomotive of history." Through revolution, those seeking to rule can repeatedly level, disrupt, and reorder society under their control, each time siphoning more wealth and power for themselves. This principle lies at the core of Hegelian Dialects. Reflecting the Confucian roots of Marxism, Confucius promulgated that society needs to be reordered and renewed constantly to achieve a "rectification of names."

The rectification of names is consistent with Plato's concept of a division of labor, that every name should be consistent with what it represents. Therefore a ruler should be an absolute ruler, and a slave an absolute slave, thus reinforcing a plutocracy.

When Confucius was alive a few thousand years ago, Central Asia was transitioning from a slave to a feudal society. Slave uprisings against the emerging landlord class resulted in continuous class struggles. The slave holding class was represented by Confucius who sought power from others who had it.

Confucianism is now actively promoted in America through Confucius Institutes, and throughout China, which requires Chinese civil servants to master Confucianism before they can can assume their place within the Communist Chinese bureaucracy. Confucius realized that in order for new power structures to be installed, the slaves needed to be mobilized to overturn an established class that did not wish to relinquish its power. The old power structure must therefore be targeted, maligned, overthrown, stripped of its assets, and eliminated so that those who wanted to have wealth and power could claim what they wanted for themselves..

Within the Confucian world view, the elite are entitled to all the wealth, power, privileges, and education in the world, and the slaves are entitled to nothing but oppression and misery.

While Confucius believed himself to be compassionate towards the less fortunate, his slaves held a different view. After the slaves rebelled in Zheng, the slave owners ruthlessly slaughtered them, leading Confucius to howl sanctimoniously, "We're so magnanimous toward our slaves, and now they just want to revolt? It would be better to seriously suppress them because only then would we be able to destroy this problem root and branch!" While preaching benevolence toward others, he said, "the benevolent only treat slaves and revolutionaries with viciousness, so that they are able to safeguard the slave-owner class."

Serving as a source for the new prosperity gospel promoted in Christian churches, Confucius said, "life and death are fated; riches and honors are due to Heaven."

Upon receiving death threats, Confucius said, "I possess the innate qualities of Heaven so I have no fear of (anyone) killing me."

The cabal that was taking shape around the Vatican and China placed no value on human life and was obsessed with maintaining its power and privilege at any cost.

After the Ming dynasty fell, the incoming Qing dynasty banned the White Lotus society on grounds that it "carried out deviant and heretical practices, met in secret places, (and) misled people under the pretext of virtue."

Yet, the Qing Emperors were far from virtuous in the conventional sense. In fact, they practiced shamanism and evoked demons. Jesuits serving in the Qing courts forged alliances with these rulers. The closer the Jesuits got to the darkness of Central Asia, the more demonic they became.

The Qing Emperor argued that its "Lord of Heaven" translated into the Jesuit concept of God. Yet, if they were one and the same, why did the Qing Emperor claim that rituals were required for worship and that sacrifices had to be made to honor God? One Jesuit, Antoine Gaubil, acknowledged that the Qings practiced Tiao Shen, or spirit jumping, a notion that Jesus rejected and which is consistent with demonic possession. The name of the game was power for the Vatican.

In North America, where the British were attempting to establish colonies of, by, and for the free people of God, Catholic missionaries and explorers were staking claims in Florida, New Mexico, Texas, Arizona, and Baja California and establishing Jesuit strongholds there.

The Qing dynasty was another Jesuit creation that followed a revolution organized by the Jesuits and Eastern Tartars (Manchus). If the Ming dynasty had restricted Jesuit movement in China, the Qings allowed them unfettered travel and access throughout the continent. According to reports from missionaries, the people who had settled into Eastern Tartary (present day Manchuria) hated the Muslims and worshiped the Buddhist lamas. Since Western and Eastern Tartary were subject to the Qing Emperor, who was controlled by Jesuits, the Vatican was convinced that "the Christian faith will be able to spread through (these lands) unhindered." French King Louis XIV even sent a representative to the Qing court, requesting permission to "go under your protection to take to China and to the Grand Tartary the lights of the true faith."

Once in power, the Qing dynasty focused on expanded its reach. After its invasion of China proper in 1644, the Manchus established control over Mongolia, Tibet, Turkestan, and Taiwan and came to rule the wealthiest, largest, and most populous empire in Asia.

The Manchu emperors simultaneously served as Emperors of the Chinese subjects, Khans of the Manchu-Mongol populations, and bodhisattvas ("enlightening beings") for the Tibetan and Mongol Buddhists. They also maintained a system of three capital cities called Central or universal cities – one in Manchuria, one in China proper, and one in inner Mongolia.

Manchurians and Mongolians believed that the Emperor could express the universality of his rule and his dominance over humanity through landscaping and architecture. The French Monarch modeled the landscaping at the Palace of Versailles after the Qing gardens and then proclaimed himself the "Sun King," who answers to no one, stating "I am the State."

During his service at the Qing court, Father Ripa described a "temple of idols which is constantly attended by a great number of Tao-she, or priests of the devil, who are all eunuchs dressed in yellow. It is to this Miao that the Emperor goes with his ladies to make sacrifices and adoration during his stay in Je-hol."

Other missionaries observed that when Chinese armies returned from battle, captives were slaughtered before the Meridian Gate as part of a human sacrifice ritual. "Beheading someone out of the Meridian Gate" has become a popular expression in China. How can the God worshiped by the Chinese rulers be the same as the Judaeo-Christian God who commands, "thou shall not kill?"

As the renowned 13th century Venetian explorer Marco Polo, observed, "the people in this part of the (world) are addicted to eating human flesh, esteeming it more delicate that any others, provided the death of the person has not been occasioned by the disease. They are the most savage race of men insomuch as when they slay their enemies in battle, they are anxious to drink their blood afterwards. They devour their flesh. The various ceremonious practices before these idols are so wicked and diabolical that it would be nothing less than an abomination to give an account of them. Putting their prisoner to death, they cook and eat the body in a convivial manner, asserting the human flesh surpasses every other in the excellence of its flavor."

The West would not be deterred as it sacrificed its Judaeo-Christian values at the altar of profits and power. The Big Game was on as Russia, England, France, and the Vatican sought to expand their respective empires into China where untold riches awaited them. Their enthusiasm led to compromise since foreign powers were required to submit to the Chinese tributary system which forced them to accept China's supremacy for access to China's coveted markets. Foreign powers seeking to engage China were required to send a tributary envoy to China to genuflect before the Chinese Emperor before establishing diplomatic and commercial relations.

II.
Viva La Revolution!

What should be clear is that most, if not all revolutions and wars have been waged by a few families for the purposes of empire building, with the long term goal of consolidating the world's wealth and power into the hands of the few. The drivers of this agenda view themselves as God-kings who are entitled to rule over humanity and enjoy the best life has to offer.

Many have gone along with the agenda since these so-called elites are perceived as being on the winning side of history. Joining them can do wonders for one's career and pocketbook, but at what price?

The global elites have plundered the world's resources, exterminated hundreds of millions, possibly billions, of people over centuries and have horded the world's treasures and knowledge for themselves. Worst of all, they don't use that knowledge to benefit mankind. They truly believe there is a ruling class – themselves – and that everyone else deserves to be dehumanized, demoralized, degraded, and ultimately, destroyed.

The Rothschilds play a key role in this sinister agenda. This banker dynasty has been described as leading the Khazarian mafia. Some have even remarked that the unusual skull shape of the Rothschild clan reflects a Royal bloodline that traces to immortal gods who inhabited the Earth during the ancient Sumerian era in Mesopotamia.

Once stripped of mystique and illusion, the truth appears. These people are simply primitive savages who exploited the Egyptian mystery schools and the strategies of Central Asian warlords for power and profit. They were only exceptional by virtue of their psychopathy. They acquired access to technologies and secrets that provided them an advantage over others and then leveraged that advantage to establish monopolies and dominance. They rigged markets to ensure they would always win, profit, and receive positive press coverage and that their rivals would lose and be destroyed.

Those who seriously challenged the Rothschilds and their interests were ruthlessly eliminated. The entire Rothschild worldview was dedicated to empowering and enriching themselves without a shred of decency, compassion, or honor. At the same time, they sought to weaken, demoralize, degrade, and oppress the people so that the chasm of wealth and privilege between themselves and everyone else would be so great that it could never be bridged. From this position, they could be perceived as gods and worshiped. In reality, they were just savages. Ordinary people were hoodwinked as they simply could not believe that devils like this even existed. The Rothschilds were masters of disguise and deception.

Many have asked where the Rothschilds came from and how its patriarch, like so many other elitists, lived life as a pauper only to be catapulted into inconceivable levels of wealth and power that eluded other mortals of his station. He must have been a plant who received private support from somewhere else.

One possibility is that the Rothschilds descended from a tribe in Central Asia called the Jainzhou Jurchens, whose chieftain was Nurhaci (1559-1626), a doppelganger for Jacob Rothschild, who may very well have been a bloodline – and the missing Rothschild link which did not identify with Judaism or Christianity, but Chinese Confucianism and Buddhism. This connection could explain why this dynasty wanted to elevate Communist China to lead the New World Order – as Asia may actually be the family's base and authentic homeland.

Nurhaci does not even look Oriental, though as Marco Polo documented in his travels, many tribes scattered throughout Central Asia, appeared white. They were not necessarily of European stock, but had light complexions and unique features. The facial features of Nurhaci are nearly identical to Rothschild – from the shape of the elongated skull to the aquiline nose, the shape of the eyes to the placement and slight angles of the eyebrows and thin lips.

Interestingly, Vice President Kamala Harris, the City of London's pick to implement the Green New Deal in the United States, has similar features. She may very well be a Rothschild bloodline too as the clan is known for siring children out of wedlock and then placing their progeny into positions of power.

Nurhaci **Jacob Rothschild**

Kamala Harris **Nathan Rothschild**

credits: (from left to right) Wikipedia Commons, Alchetron, Ms Magazine, One World of Nations, book jacket.

Also, consistent with a Rothschild connection, Nurhaci owed his position to the Jesuits and secret societies; his dynasty entertained both British and French Monarch. He also launched a civil service administration exam in which applicants were required to demonstrate their mastery of Confucianism before they could serve in the Chinese government.

Confucianism is the philosophical basis for Marxism and endless revolution – that of using peasants, proletariats, among other aggrieved victim classes – to overthrow the so-called privileged, loot victims, and purge populations in order to establish a more "fair and just" society. The new republic that emerges from the violence appears on the surface to be more democratic but is controlled from the shadows by a ruling elite. Through each revolution and war, more wealth and power is consolidated within the hands of the elite.

The pattern has been repeated ad nauseam until Rothschild and his allies wound up controlling the Vatican, the City of London, the British Monarchy, Central Banks, most governments, most, if not all, Royal families, Israel, the United States, and Communist China. Those who have wrestled free from Rothschild control, including, for example, Russian and Chinese nationalists, have been identified as threats and targeted for destruction. Nations attempting to act independently and in their own interests within a globalist system are targeted for war and regime change.

The world view the Rothschilds embraced was that of a hierarchy with an elite (themselves) in control and everyone else serving them. In order to reinforce their elite status as God-kings, they must demonstrably prove their superiority by dehumanizing and degrading those over which they rule.

These are the people who have used extermination events as military tactics to remove people or groups of people seen as obstacles to their plans so that their agenda can move forward unencumbered, as reflected in tactics employed by the East India Company. The Rothschilds have seized valuable art and treasures from their victims, celebrated their homicidal tyrants as heroes, and horded wealth and secret technologies, also consistent with Qing tactics. They created unfavorable trade arrangements that placed themselves first and others in their debt.

When not otherwise pirating and engaging in war, the Qing

dynasty employed ruthless, self-serving tactics that were absorbed by the Hanseatic League, which became the template for Rothschild's European Union. The Hanseatic League engaged in trade with these Central Asian tribes, centering around the textile trade in Germany whose textile manufacturers, like Friedrich Engels, migrated over to British industrial cities, like Manchester, and fomented Marxist-style revolutions, supported and driven by Rothschild agents trained at the Tavistock Institute.

The textile trade, along with banking, served as their vehicle for market dominance, no doubt accounting for the modeling industry's exploitation of people, consistent with the sickness demonstrated by merchants doing business in Central Asia. Jeffrey Epstein, who procured children for Royal families, celebrities, and other high level Rothschild assets, tapped the fashion world for underage prostitutes who were reportedly treated not only as sex objects, but slaves.

Who were among the first promoters and defenders of human trafficking? The East India Company (EIC) and merchants who partnered with Central Asia mercenaries, and Rothschild. Who brought the institution of slavery to America that had been rejected by Christians? Rothschild and merchants engaged in commerce with Central Asia.

The tactics employed by the Chinese nobility resemble those of the Rothschilds – that of amassing private wealth through taxation; promoting one rule for the elite, another for the slaves; stirring up perpetual war and revolution; promoting globalism to expand their empires. The Rothschilds simply carried out a centuries old agenda from Central Asia, with Jerusalem to link Europe, Africa, Asia, and the Middle East in trade and commerce through a Silk Road.

The Hanseatic League acquired its wealth and power through the silk trade, based upon trading routes established between China and Europe. In fact, the Silk Road derives its name from the German term, Seidenstraße, which literally means "Silk Road." The Rothschild patriarch launched his banking career in Frankfurt, Germany, providing loans and financial advice to merchants and Royal families.

The Rothschilds have served as a gateway into the lucrative Chinese markets from which the Hanseatic League and Europe's wealthiest merchants owe much of their wealth.

Whether the Rothschild are related to Nurhaci is up for speculation. However, the Rothschilds have followed the Qing agenda and strategies to the letter.

The Rothschild also adopted the symbolism of the Jesuit's Knight Templar – that of the red cross, which has come to symbolize Jesuit conquest. They dropped their family name (Bauer) to adopt a name that literally means red cross (Rothschild). Under the banner of Christianity, the Knights Templar raped, murdered, and robbed innocent people while providing pilgrims safe passage to Jerusalem. Governments didn't make concessions to the Rothschilds and its revolutionaries based upon any innate superiority or talent the Rothschilds and their allies might have had but rather that they were unprepared for the barbarism, treachery, and unrestrained evil and greed that they displayed.

When governments were threatened with Rothschild-sponsored wars, they found themselves having no choice but to go to the banking family that somehow had the resources to give them loans, not understanding that this family and its aligned networks were bankrolling all sides of wars and revolutions and then manipulating outcomes through their extensive intelligence and secret society networks. Nobody could ever have conceived that such a people existed, not in civilized Europe anyway, particularly as the Rothschilds looked and acted like one of them – a civilized European who happened to be banker and advisor to Monarchs and the Vatican.

The Rothschilds eventually insinuated themselves into the British and European Royal families, into the Vatican, and into the American establishment, placing their bloodlines and agents into key positions of power, eventually controlling the City of London (global finance), the Vatican (global religion), and the United States (global military and ATM machine).

Unlike the typical robber baron, the Central Asian tribes were willing to exterminate millions of people, topple governments, and destroy humanity to reach their goals, not caring about the impact their actions had upon others as they believed they were entitled to whatever they wanted and that humanity had no value beyond that which it provided to them. People existed to serve them and then perish.

Nurhaci evoked demons to protect his clan, the Aisin Gioro, and destroy rivals. His clan was one of three major groups of the

Jurchens – who trace to Liaonig, China, a small coastal province located on the northern shore of the Yellow Sea which served as a gateway between China proper and Manchuria. Known as the Golden Triangle, Lianoing linked to the Korea Bay and Bohai Sea in the south, and North Korea's Pyongan and Chagang provinces. Lianoing, also known as Yan, was at the center of numerous maritime, diplomatic, and trade missions which traded extensively with the Venetians and other powerful merchant families connected to the Vatican.

The Jurchens were known for keeping the industrial secrets for dying cloth, which spurred the Hanseatic League's industry once Europeans acquired a taste and demand for exotic textures from China, like silk and noncombustible materials made from salamander. The clan remained close to key trading towns like Fushan, Kaiyuan, Tieling, and Manpojin, helping to spur the League's power and influence. These routes were among the trade routes of the Venetians who partnered with barbarian horde mercenaries, to establish market dominance, eliminate rivals, and serve in the Crusades on behalf of powerful Italian merchant families and the Vatican, who sought to conquer Jerusalem for the Papacy.

The Jianzhou Jurchen deceptively changed their name to Manchu to hide the fact that they were not God's chosen rulers or even the descendants of gods, but the conquered subjects of the Chinese. To cloak their real identities, the Qing dynasty hid books, like *Taizu Shily Tu,* in the Qing palace within the Forbidden City. *The History of Ming* also documents that the Jurchens were below the Ming dynasty on the social hierarchy.

From the beginning, they were pretenders who claimed titles, wealth, privileges, and accomplishments which didn't belong to them. Translated literally in the Manchu language, Nurhaci, the head of the Jurchen clan, means "the skin of a wild boar."

Nurhaci placed shamanism, or demon worship, at the center of his state's rituals; he made sacrifices to Heaven before setting off to battle. His son, Hong Taiji (1592-1643), who renamed the Jurchens "Manchu," founded the Qing dynasty from 1636 – around the time the Pilgrims were establishing a society of, by and for the free people of God in North America.

At the same time, the early colonial societies were being infiltrated by subversive elements from the East India Company, which had business before the Qing court. The Qing dynasty evoked demons in service of the state – while forbidding others to have knowledge of these practices or even to engage in them.

The Qing dynasty's Qianlong Emperor Hongli (1735-1796), who assumed the throne around the time the French and American Revolutions, commissioned the publication of a "Shamanic Code" to regulate shamanism and ensure its secrets and powers remained the preserve of the Qing dynasty by destroying rival shrines. Through military aggression, the Qianlong Emperor expanded the Qing empire throughout China, destroying other Central Asia kingdoms in the process.

A British valet who accompanied a diplomat to the Qing court in 1793 described Hongli as "about five feet ten inches in height, and of a slender, but elegant form; his complexion is comparatively fair, though his eyes are dark; his nose is rather aquiline, and the whole of his countenance presents a perfect regularity of feature, which, by no means, announce the great age he is said to have attained; his person is attractive, and his deportment accompanied by an affability, which, without lessening the dignity of the prince, evinces the amiable character of the man. His dress consisted of a loose robe of yellow silk, a cap of black velvet with a red ball on the top, and adorned with a peacock's feather, which is the peculiar distinction of mandarins of the first class. He wore silk boots embroidered with gold, and a sash of blue girded his waist."

Intercepted Jesuit letters paint a picture of an Emperor with no clothes. One Jesuit described the Qianlong Emperor's journey to Chengde was as a "bumbling comedy of errors." While the Emperor thought of himself as a bodhisattva, the Jesuits in his service viewed him as a comically narcissistic, uncompromising task master.

The correspondence of missionaries in the service of the Emperor provide a fascinating glimpse into the culture surrounding the early Qing dynasty, including the incessant feuding among warlords, the corrupt mandarins who embezzled from state coffers, and the penchant of the Emperor to confer great luxury, wealth, and powers upon loyal subjects, perhaps accounting for why so many were eager to get into his good graces. As Father Amiot observed:

At long last a revolution occurred in the country of the

Zunghars among the Tartar sovereign whose states are bordered in the middle by Tibet; bordered on the east by Tartars who are the tributaries of China, the Khalkhas and the Mongols; bordered on the west by Muslim Tartars and nomads; and bordered on the north by a part of Siberia.

After the death of the last Zunghar, a lama of royal blood placed himself at the head of a powerful faction and came finally to be recognized despite his contenders, particularly those who wanted, naturally, to occupy the throne.

This new sovereign, an agitated and turbulent man, fearless and inflated with his first successes, wanted new conquests and he was confident in his ability and good fortune.

He found it distasteful that the Khalkhas, his neighbors, were tributaries of China, and he convinced himself of subjugating them.

He submitted to the Emperor the ridiculous proposition that the (Emperor) cede them to him, alleging that it was a right owed to his crown that Zunghars of old had enjoyed and alleging that he was well resolved to employ all his forces in order to enjoy them himself.

The Emperor responded to these pretensions only by inviting him to become a tributary of the empire, offering to make him an official of the first rank and maintain him upon his throne.

The lama-become-Zunghar felt his pride offended at such a proposition. He responded that he was in his state as sovereign as the Emperor was in his, that he cared nothing for official rank, that he was declaring war, and that arms would decide who of the two would receive homage and tribute from the Khalkhas.

Of course there were many malcontents among the subjects of the usurper, and as their discontent was only waiting for a favorable occasion to explode, the most enlightened of them concluded that they must profit from the good will that they supposed the Emperor would show to those who declared themselves enemies of that tyrant.

They secretly formed the plot; ten thousand of them fled their country and came with their families and all their baggage to present themselves before the Emperor and recognize him as their sovereign and master.

The Emperor received them with open arms; he gave them a site in Chinese Tartary where he permitted them to establish themselves.

He named some mandarins to check to see that they did not lack anything – or, more likely, to check on what they were doing. He sent them great sums of money and provisions of all kinds in great quantity; in a word, he put them in a position to lead in their new home much more comfortable lives than they had enjoyed in their own country.

Interestingly, the so-called "Aryan" master race were the nobles of Iran/India, the mandarins, the very people upon whose behalf German Fuhrer, Adolf Hitler, a Rothschild bloodline, led his bloody campaign against Jews and gypsies during World War II. The Nazi symbol adorns Tibetan shrines, a Buddhist symbol for good luck. Hitler and the Nazis also took trips to the Arctic and Tibet to acquire knowledge of secret technologies that they could use against humanity.

In correspondence, one missionary wrote that the Emperor "was surrounded by luxuries indicating that he had accumulated much merit in previous lives. His queens were wearing white brocade robes. He considered himself the ruler of the Earth and a great leader with many intimidating army battalions."

The genocidal nature of the Qings was apparent early on. For example, after the Dzungar Khanate (renamed Xinjiang) was incorporated into the Qing Empire, Hongli ordered the genocide of the Dzungar (Kunghars), a coalition of Western Mongol tribes. One scholar, Wei Yuan, reported that 40 percent of the 600,000 Kunghars died of small pox, a disease that was similarly used to exterminate the Native-Americans. The surviving Kunghars fled to Russia where Soviet premier Joseph Stalin, a Rothschild bloodline, finished them off through genocide.

Chemical warfare was used by the East India Company as a military tactic once it became an imperialist force. After Rothschild acquired control of Great Britain through the Napoleonic Wars, British imperialists engaged in genocide through chemical warfare to expand the British Empire. If a group of people proved inconvenient, troublesome, or needed to be forcibly removed from land, people were exterminated, run into concentration camps, or enslaved.

Once under Rothschild control, the City of London became an unrelenting source of evil in which an elite sought to consolidate the world's wealth and power within its own hands. Rothschild reportedly lamented the idealistic nature of ordinary Brits who thought they could spread the light of Christianity and civilization around the world for the honor of the British Empire. Rothschild was only interested in the business at hand – that of conquest, execution, and plunder. The conquerors even used famine as a weapon, as evidenced in Ireland, the Ukraine, and elsewhere.

In 1776, just as the American Revolution was getting underway, the Qing exterminated the Jinchuan Tibetan people. After the slaughter, the victorious troops returned to Beijing and sang a celebratory hymn in their own honor.

When the Khalkha Mongol rebels aligned with the Kunghars against the Qing Empire, the Qing army crushed the rebellion and executed the Mongolian prince and his entire family in a manner reminiscent of the execution of the Russian Romanovs, who were lined up against a wall and shot by Bolsheviks, revolutionary forces drawn from Central Asia. As Karl Marx said, "We have no compassion, and we ask no compassion from you. When our turn comes, we shall not make excuses for the terror."

As Tibetan Buddhism spread throughout Mongolia, the Qianlong Emperor sent armies into Tibet and installed the Dalai Lama as Tibetan ruler. The Dalai Lama, who evoked demons, became the spiritual advisor to the House of Windsor after Rothschild installed the dynasty with his bloodline, Queen Elizabeth II, as figurehead. Rebels who resisted Qing control were sliced to death at the hands of Qing Manchu General Bandi; their property was then seized and placed under the control of the Qing dynasty. As Marx wrote in the *Communist Manifesto*, "In one word, you reproach us with intending to do away with your property. Precisely so: that is just what we intend."

In a separate incident, the Uyghur Muslims rebelled against the Qing after the Manchu official Su-cheng, his servants, and son gang raped Uyghur women for months. The outraged Ush Muslims reportedly sought to kill and cannibalize the rapists. The Qianlong Emperor responded by ordering the massacre of the entire Uyghur town, stipulating that the men be slaughtered and the women and children be enslaved.

The Qing Empire began to fray at the seams as a result of

corrupt, brutal leaders, internal infighting, and corruption. Its elites had become so wealthy and comfortable that they neglected to to train their armies or exert effort to do much of anything, rendering them weak and ineffectual.

The Qianlong Emperor sought to fortify his empire by establishing a replica of the Tibetan Potala Palace in Chengde with copper and gold tiled roofs. Even though he had massacred Buddhists, the Emperor portrayed himself as a bodhisattva and then hid his Confucian leanings in order to win favor with the people he had attacked.

He even commissioned a painting of himself as Manjushri, the bodhisattva of wisdom. As one historian observed: "Over his shoulder to the right is a book, and to the left is the sword of wisdom which cuts through ignorance. His right hand is in the teaching mudra. Qianlong wears the pandita's hat, and in his left hand carries the wheel of Buddhist teaching that marks him as the dharmaraja, a great ruler who turns the wheels of the Buddhist teachings, and the inscription reinforces this ideal: To the human lord (Qianlong) who is the sharp (minded) Manjushri manifesting as the great owner of the world and Dharmaraja. The emperor-bodhisattva is surrounded by 108 deities representing the lineage of humans and deities linked in transmitting particular Buddhist teachings from teacher to disciple. The Tibetan lama in the circle above Qianlong's nimbus is his root teacher. Others in the assembly include a tutelary deity who annihilates death, a main deity of the major tantric initiation."

The bottom portion of the painting displays three main deities who are protectors of Tibetan Buddhism and Tibet – including Yama, the lord of death; the six-armed Mahakala; and Palden Lhamo, the protectoress of Tibet. The Dalai Lama is depicted as ruler of Tibet.

Reminiscent of a Rothschild mansion, the Emperor's palace "contained over 100,000 volumes of scriptures and historical documents" and "many store rooms for housing precious objects, handicrafts, printings, wall hangings, statues, and ancient armor." Both the palace and temple managed to escape damage during the Cultural Revolution which was led by Rothschild bloodline Chairman Mao Tse-tung.

The Qianlong Emperor was a major patron and important "preserver and restorer" of Confucian culture, the basis for cultural

Marxism; he also possessed an insatiable appetite for acquiring China's "great private collections" to add to his "imperial collection." He also enjoyed pressuring wealthy courtiers into surrendering their art to him and then squirreled away his possessions behind the walls of the Forbidden City.

Even though the greatest criminal around was the man in the mirror, he sought to impose harsh penalties on Muslims for engaging in criminal behavior. Muslims needed to be treated more harshly than others, he believed, as he considered their religion "foolish."

He also ordered the Solons, who lived in Inner Mongolia, to surrender their guns to the government so that they would not be able to resist his tyranny effectively.

A friend of the Vatican, the Qianlong Emperor commissioned Giuseppe Castiglione, an Italian Jesuit, to construct a Western style mansion for him. A French Jesuit by the name of Michel Benoist was enlisted to design fountains and waterworks with underground machinery and pipes to entertain the Emperor and his family. Benoist worked alongside Castiglione to transform the Emperor's Old Summer Palace into an "imitation of the Palace of Versailles," which was designed to reinforce the French Royal family's power through imposing architecture and elaborate garden designs. The Emperor told the Jesuit craftsmen that if they didn't complete the construction projects before deadline, he'd have them executed.

Castiglione and Benoist also constructed European-style pavilions at the Old Summer Palace that included elaborate hydraulics for fountains, including a "water lock" in front of the Hall of Calm Seas, which was inspired by the Palace of Versailles; each clock consisted of a fountain surrounded by 12 statues depicting the animals of the Chinese zodiac. French King Louis XV gifted the Emperor copper engravings in keeping with French themes.

The Emperor shared Rothschild's passion for the Palace of Versailles. As the *Tatler* reported in 2019, "The Rothschilds have always been passionate about two things: wine and art," just like the Qing Emperors. "In 1853, original wine-connoisseur Baron Nathaniel de Rothschild bought the Château Brane-Mouton in Bordeaux at auction in order to serve his own wine to his prestigious guests, with the estate becoming Château Mouton Rothschild ever after. Now, the latest generation to helm the winery has teamed up with leading artists of today to design a special case of bottles to be auctioned this spring to raise money for the restoration of the Palace of Versailles."

The Rothschilds were so enamored with collecting art that after Marie Antoinette was guillotined during the French Revolution, her private desk was installed in a Rothschild mansion. "This thrilling partnership with the Palace of Versailles is an extension of our commitment to and support for the arts," the Rothschilds announced in promotional materials.

By the 18th century, the Jesuits were facing retaliation for their subversive activities after European Emperors concluded that they were abusing their power and acquiring too much money.

In 1724, the role of the Jesuit missionaries was reinvented to realign their focus from spreading the Christian faith for the Vatican to learning and documenting Manchu and Chinese languages and culture for the Qianlong Emperor.

As historians observed, the Qianlong Emperor worked with Jesuits to spread the rational Enlightenment, which was based upon Asian logic and the teachings of Greek philosophers Plato and Aristotle, and Chinese ideologies, like Confucianism, and Buddhism. The rational Enlightenment sowed the seeds of destruction in Europe, for the purposes of conquest. European monarchs and societies were to be destabilized and overthrown. Aristocrats and Royals who had once modeled good, noble behavior for the public descended to debauchery, lewdness, and unrestrained sensation-seeking. As Monarchies fell, republics took their place. These republics were based upon Plato's *Republic* – that of a plutocracy, or government of the few ruling the many.

While the Jesuits were being suppressed in Europe, they had gained influence at the Qing court. So enamored was the Milan-born Jesuit Castiglione of China that he changed his name to Lang Shi'ning.

At the beginning of the 18th century, European powers pressured China for opportunities to trade, but the Qianlong Emperor resisted on grounds that he had all the wealth and resources he could ever possibly want. If foreign countries wanted to do business with him, they would have to make more concessions and submit to more demands and then maybe he would reconsider.

In 1793, King George III sent a delegation to present his request for trade concessions directly to the Emperor in Beijing through his diplomat, George Macartney, who brought with him goods that Britain hoped to sell in China. Since Chinese rulers demanded tribute from foreigners, the Emperor misinterpreted Mcartney's products as tribute and then flew into a rage over being presented goods of inferior quality that did not sufficiently recognize his God-like stature.

The Emperor believed that he presided over a Celestial Empire in which the entire world revolved around him and his "great central kingdom." No one thought as highly of the Qianlong Emperor as he thought of himself. After rejecting Macartney's proposal, the Emperor wrote to King George III:

Yesterday your Ambassador petitioned my Ministers to memorialize me regarding your trade with China, but his proposal is not consistent with our dynastic usage and cannot be entertained. Hitherto, all European nations, including your own country's barbarian merchants, have carried on their trade with our Celestial Empire at Canton. Such has been the procedure for many years, although our Celestial Empire possesses all things in prolific abundance and lacks no product within its own borders.

Your request for a small island near Chusan, where your merchants may reside and goods be warehoused, arises from your desire to develop trade. Consider, moreover, that England is not the only barbarian land which wishes to establish trade with our Empire: supposing that other nations were all to imitate your evil example and beseech me to present them each and all with a site for trading purposes, how could I possibly comply? This also is a flagrant infringement of the usage of my Empire and cannot possibly be entertained.

Hitherto, the barbarian merchants of Europe have had a definite locality assigned to them at Aomen for residence and trade, and have been forbidden to encroach an inch beyond the limits assigned to that locality. If these restrictions were withdrawn, friction would inevitably occur between the Chinese and your barbarian subjects.

Regarding your nation's worship of the Lord of Heaven, it is the same religion as that of other European nations. Ever since the beginning of history, sage Emperors and wise rulers have bestowed on

China a moral system and inculcated a code, which from time immemorial has been religiously observed by the myriad of my subjects. There has been no hankering after heterodox doctrines. Even the European (missionary) officials in my capital are forbidden to hold intercourse with Chinese subjects.

In his own memoirs, Macartney wrote that the Qing Emperor was "an old, crazy, first-rate Man of War, which a fortunate succession of able and vigilant officers have contrived to keep afloat for these hundred and fifty years past, and to overawe their neighbors merely by his bulk and appearance. But whenever an insufficient man happens to have the command on deck, adieu to the discipline and safety of the ship. She may, perhaps, not sink outright; she may drift some time as a wreck, and will then be dashed to pieces on the shore; but she can never be rebuilt on the old bottom."

A Dutch diplomatic mission traveled to the Qianlong Emperor in 1795, making this the last time any European would appear before the Qing imperial court.

In 1776, the Qianlong Emperor moved out of the Hall of Mental Cultivation in the Forbidden City which had been dedicated to his exclusive use as reigning sovereign. In 1771, as stirrings of revolution got underway in North America, construction was begun on his retirement retreat at the Palace of Tranquin Longevity in Qianlong Garden.

In October of 1795, the Qianlong Emperor announced that he would resign the following year – right after the French ratified a national constitution at the Constitutional Convention, which ended the French revolution and marked the ascendancy of Napoleon Bonaparte, whose assault on Europe resulted in the fall of the Holy Roman Empire, England, France, and Vatican into the hands of Rothschild who bankrolled and managed all sides of the war.

The Emperor was rumored to be the son of Chen Shiguan, the governor of the Confucius home province of Shandong who later became a leading proponent of Confucianism.

Like others in Central Asia, he practiced shamanistic rituals and worshiped a number of Gods including the bodhisattva. He also reprimanded Manchu converts to Christianity for worshiping the "Lord of Heaven," rather than practicing shamanism and demon worship, "the spiritual core of Manchu life." As the Emperor explained, "In the empire, we have a temple for honoring Heaven and sacrificing to him. We Manchus have Tiao Tehin." (A court Jesuit, Antoine Gaubil, described Tiao Tehin as "spirit jumping," or demon possession.)

Strict controls were imposed on Mongols with regards to climate change, which refers to changes in the "conditions of the physical and human environment."

The Qings demanded harmony between Heaven and human society – that is, between the rulers and ruled, with the ruled accepting their enslavement with calm passivity.

The Qing dynasty set up a Court of Colonial Affairs, which managed relations with Mongols, Muslims, Tibetans, Russians, and other ethnic groups under Qing control.

The Court evolved into a Ministry of Foreign Affairs and ultimately, the Foreign Office, which managed tributes, border disputes, military affairs, justice, citizen registrations, taxes, the economy, trade, and religion.

In a manner reminiscent of the Rothschilds, the Qings passed along its wives and daughters to colleagues to enhance their diplomatic relations. One Westerner observed that the Qings "took to their beds those who are cousins by blood and even their own cousins. Many other moral sins are regarded by them with indifference, and they live in this respect like beasts in the field." As is widely known, the Rothschilds are kissing cousins. They notoriously marry within the family to ensure the money doesn't leave outside of it and then spawn Rothschild bastards through third parties, like maids and stable boys; these children are then elevated to positions of prominence as secret Rothschilds.

In *Folktales from Chengde,* "The Dragons on the Roof of the Travel Palace Temple" speaks to the practice of sacrificing children "to the furnace" to complete a temple to welcome a Tibetan Panchen Living Buddha coming to pay his respects to the Qianlong Emperor.

There were also reports of human hunting parties to demonstrate Qing dominance over conquered subjects. Hunting was the preserve of the elite who equated hunting with war. Their hunts were always performed in a ritualistic fashion. One Jesuit referred to the Manchu hunting tradition as an "adaptation of an older practice for newer purposes." Hunting came to be associated with the "sport of

Kings," with elites posting pictures of themselves smiling over the corpses of dead animals.

To reinforce its power, the Qing dynasty staged annual imperial hunting parties. As one historian observed: "The hunts were large scale exercises involving thousands of men divided into smaller units who fanned out to encircle a large area of forest. As the circle was drawn tighter, the game was driven out into the open where it presented a better target. Of course, animals were also more dangerous under these circumstances, and participants in the hunt had to demonstrate bravery and good horsemanship to avoid injury while keeping cornered beasts from escaping. Any who failed this test were subject to punishment."

This was a dynastic tradition of Inner Asian elites, with the emperor participating along with thousands of soldiers, imperial family members, and government officials.

The Qing elite left the Forbidden City and hunted as their ancestors had done for generations. The hunts were ritualized to preserve the Manchu way of life. Representatives of tributary states were required to participate on a rotating basis.

Human hunting and sacrifices were linked to the new aristocracy and Chinese elite. As an historian observed: "To employ against a human enemy the same patience and valor, the same skill and discipline is the only altercation which is required in real war, and the amusements of the chase serves as a prelude to the conquest of an empire."

The ultimate goal of the Qing dynasty was "universal rule based upon submissions of divergent people whose culture would remain separate."

The Opium Wars would derails these ambitions, but Rothschild picked up where the Qings left off. In the 19th century, French and British troops reached the Palace to negotiate Qing surrender. By this point, Britain and France were controlled by Rothschild. The Emperor responded by imprisoning and torturing the delegation, killing twenty.

At the direction of the British High Commissioner to China, Lord Elgin, the Qing palace was destroyed by British troops – but not before the sculptures, porcelain, jade, silk robes, elaborate textiles, and gold were hauled away and sent to nearly four dozen museums around the world. Befitting a pattern of Rothschild looting, Lord Elgin, as Ambassador to Constantinople, removed entire boatloads of ancient sculpture from Athens, including sculptures from the Parthenon and seventeen life-size marble figures. The loot was then displayed at the British Museum in London.

In 1842, Queen Victoria signed the Treaty of Nanking with the Emperor of China, a surprisingly unequal treaty in which Britain had extracted major concessions from China while offering nothing in return. Britain even won "most favored nation" status with China and was granted extraterritorial rights. The British also acquired the right to negotiate directly with local officials, with China ceding the island of Hong Kong to Britain. China paid war reparations in the amount of $21 million. By this time, Rothschild controlled all of Britain, its banks, and Monarchy and so was consolidating power in London. The Rothschilds took control of England, and then England took control of China, solidifying the Rothschild empire. The Emperor had been propped up by Jesuits who worked for the Vatican, which answered to Rothschild.

The Treaty of Tientsin of 1858, allowed Britain, France, Russia, and the United States to open embassies in Peking (Beijing). Additional ports were then opened to accommodate foreign traders, allowing them to travel into China, with China forced once again to pay indemnities. By this point, the Rothschilds were attempting to consolidate their control over China so that China could be elevated to to lead the New World Order.

III.
Chinese Takeout

While attempting to claim North America for the Vatican, Catholic missionaries and explorers surveyed the land, identifying and recording mountain ranges, rivers, ports, and other assets for the purposes of helping merchants establish new lines of trade with China from the West coast. Missionaries who joined these teams set up farms and ports guarded by armed forces.

Meanwhile, the Jesuits were wrecking havoc throughout Europe by running campaigns for Chinese leaders who believed themselves to be God-Kings, or living gods, a status to which the Jesuits aspired. The Chinese leaders, in turn, were inspired by Confucianism, a moral system based upon moral relativism and rational self-interest which reinforced a social hierarchy in which the few ruled the many.

Throughout Central Asia and Europe, the Jesuits were fomenting Confucian (Marxist)-style revolutions to reorganize society under the control of the elite. Through each reorganization, they plundered the wealth and treasures of the fallen. The tactic was effective and simple, and the power they accumulated, intoxicating. Christian Monarchs were appalled by the tactics, leading Jesuits to fall out of favor in Christian kingdoms. Some Jesuits went underground while others remained in China.

While serving Chinese rulers, the Jesuits fomented dissent between Catholic Monarchs and their colonies in North America. They also played a behind-the-scenes role in the American Revolution. Cognizant of the foreign machinations and intrigue surrounding him, General George Washington, America's first President, took measures to protect his country, but the young, idealistic nation remained a target as this was the only country in the world created of, by and for the free people of God.

While the colonists enjoyed amicable relations with the Indians, the Jesuits had already established relationships with them – decades, even centuries earlier, through military and commercial posts. As the colonists attempted to move west of the Appalachian Mountains, the Indians were weaponized against them.

As a free people, the Americans weren't like the order-following hordes of Central Asia. They moved onward with God serving as a lamp unto their feet. Through the Indian tribes, the shadow elite aspired to put an end to "individualistic white America" and usher social democracy into the United States. A free, independently-minded people couldn't be controlled, the Vatican and Central Asian leaders quickly learned, so in order to control them, the people had to be rendered weak through taxation (tribute), and made dependent so that they would have no choice but to obey, like cattle. Attacks would eventually be levied against Americans from all directions to render them exploitable for the purposes of conquest.

Among the most unscrupulous of the Founding Fathers was Benjamin Franklin, an inventor, philosopher, and diplomat to the Court of St. James in London. By some accounts, this Hellfire Club member was engaging in human sacrifice. He also helped instigate the French Revolution to remove the French Monarch and aristocracy from power so that an aspiring ruling class, with ties to China, could emerge from the shadows and claim the wealth, power, and influence of the targeted French aristocrats for themselves.

Yet, Franklin is among the most celebrated of the Founding Fathers. His name graces Franklin Templeton, a global investment firm founded in 1947, which reportedly holds assets in excess of $1.4 trillion; Franklin Templeton is listed on the New York Stock Exchange under BEN in honor of his memory. Franklin's face also graces the $100 bill, the largest denomination of America's currency, perhaps reflecting the esteem he still holds among the secret societies and global financial elite.

Franklin was the nation's first Post Master General. The U.S. Postal Service was modeled after the postal system in Central Asia which helped warlords and merchants shore up markets, eliminate competition, and spy on rivals. The USPS was the beginning of the surveillance society in the United States.

To this day, the Chinese praise Franklin for being "very fond of reading about China." According to historians, Franklin explored every aspect of China, from its spiritual roots to its material aspects. He eagerly promoted Confucian moral philosophy and introduced Chinese industrial technologies into America. Of particular interest to Franklin were opportunities to make silk and produce gun powder. "The

European silk is all yellow as is most of the Indian silk," Franklin observed. "What comes from China is white."

Gun power was reportedly created by the Chinese after Emperor Wu Di of the Han dynasty (156-87 BC) directed his alchemists to concoct an elixir for immortality. They came up with interesting chemical combinations that, during the Tang dynasty of the 8th century, helped the Chinese invent gunpowder and fireworks!

In correspondence, Franklin wrote that Confucius was his inspiration and role model. He preached virtues that appeared consistent with Christianity, like frugality and industriousness. However, the rabble-rousing revolutionaries supported an ideology that led to the execution of French Monarchs and aristocrats and to the seizure of their assets. After studying Confucianism, Franklin established "a systematic approach to virtue that emphasized a gradual bit-by-bit approach toward perfection," or the Buddhist notion of enlightenment known as the rational Enlightenment.

According to Franklin's autobiography, the 13 virtues he espoused were based upon *The Morals of Confucius*. Franklin preached temperance, that one should not "eat for pleasure," but "eat to increase thy strength, to preserve the life which thou has received from Heaven." At the same time, he denied the existence of a God. According to missionaries, the Chinese leaders ate the bodies of those who had passed before in order to acquire the substance of that person. Consuming a person with great personal attributes, like wisdom or strength, for example, ensured that those traits were passed on to others, missionaries observed while serving in the Chinese courts. This practice may explain why the corpses of 15 people were found buried in a basement in a windowless room beneath a garden at Franklin's residence in London. Cannibalism and blood drinking were rituals used by the Asiatic elite and their priests to facilitate spirit jumping and demon possession.

While Franklin promoted frugality, he engaged in conspicuous consumption. Placed within the context of the rational Enlightenment, riches were obtained through theft, war, and outright plunder, as was demonstrated during the French Revolution. For elites, frugality meant parsimony.

The illegitimate elite horde the wealth and treasures they have plundered from others and avoid taxes while imposing taxes on others.

They demand tribute while withholding payments. They cultivate dependency – and after looting public treasuries, ration entitlements. In the interests of frugality, dependents are told that there simply isn't enough money to go around, that they must tighten their belts and live with less.

"What assurances of the future can be better found than that which is built on experience of the past," Franklin proclaimed. This would be all well and good if he hadn't based his experience upon genocidal tyrants who worshiped themselves as God, enslaved people, and practiced demonic possession.

Franklin looked to the Chinese to develop the American way of life and founded the American Philosophical Society with this goal in mind. "Could we be so fortunate as to introduce the industry of the Chinese, their arts of living and improvements in husbandry, as well as their native plants, America might be as populous as China, which is allowed to contain more inhabitants than any other country in the world," Franklin said.

"The American dream started with China," said Dr. David Wang, Adjunct Professor of St. Johns University. "Even before the colonists landed, Chinese influence had begun. The Virginia Company supported the exploration of North America. The company had to choose where to place the landing. It wanted to land somewhere close to a place from which it could get to China."

For the record, the American dream did not start with China. It started with the Pilgrims, a free people who worshiped God and who were sent to the North American continent by Queen Elizabeth I for the purposes of establishing a new, experimental Judaeo-Christian society.

The Virginia Company was not established by Queen Elizabeth I, who held the divine right (rite) to rule, but King James I, under whose watch the East India Company (EIC) transformed into an imperialist force. By this point, the EIC was already an agency for Chinese interests – or at least merchants seeking access to these markets.

The Virginia Company was a successor to Sir. Water Raleigh's lost colony of Roanoke, which was established in 1585 as the first permanent English settlement in North America. However, this colony never got off the ground as its population simply vanished, with nobody being able to account for what happened to them.

What was going on at the Vatican around this time? Pope Gregory XIII, who established the Gregorian calendar, was bankrolling Jesuit efforts to attack Protestants and plotting to overthrow Queen Elizabeth I.

Five years earlier, on the advice of English Jesuits, Pope Gregory XIII suspended a bull to excommunicate Queen Elizabeth so that English Catholics could remove her when the timing was right. Until such time, they were to feign support for the Queen so that their intentions would not be known.

Pope Sixtus, a member of the Franciscan order, succeeded Gregory XIII as Pope and promptly excommunicated Queen Elizabeth I; he also directed the Spanish Armada to invade England. In *An Admonition to the Nobility and People of England and Ireland,* Cardinal William Allen challenged the Queen's legitimacy, calling her "an incestuous bastard, begotten and born in sin of an infamous courtesan Anne Boleyn," the wife of King Henry VIII, who had broken with the Catholic Church to establish the Church of England.

Within this context, did the Jesuits have motive and opportunity to sabotage Raleigh's Roanoke colony to prevent a Protestant Queen from establishing a foothold in North America? Absolutely! The Pilgrims and early colonists pursued and established the American dream. They did not wish to be controlled by the Vatican or conform to Confucian principles. Nor did they support a nascent government whose allegiance was to the Pope, a distant Chinese Emperor, Jesuits, or Rothschild-affiliated bankers. Rather, they were Christians and Jews who believed in God and prided themselves in being independent, sovereign individuals who were equal under God and who enjoyed rights, privileges, and freedoms enumerated in the U.S. Constitution and Bill of Rights. They were self-reliant and enterprising, qualities that put them at odds with those who sought to put an end to "individualistic white America."

In 1529, Queen Elizabeth I granted a charter for Sir Humphrey Gilbert to explore and colonize territories unclaimed by Christian kingdoms north of Spanish Florida.

After Gilbert's death, the Queen divided the charter between his brother, Adrian; and his half brother, Sir Walter Raleigh. Adrian's charter gave him the patent for Newfoundland for the purposes of charting a path to Asia. Raleigh was awarded the lands to the south and was named King, Lord, and Governor of Virginia, a state he named after his beloved virgin Queen.

Raleigh sought investors and planned a military operation focused on exploring and evaluating Virginia's natural resources. While some six hundred men reportedly accompanied him on his first voyage, as soon as the colonists arrived, many fell victim to a deadly epidemic, like smallpox.

The nascent Virginia Company was attempting to establish a landing "somewhere close to a place where it could get to China," Wang wrote. "France supported the American Revolution. Why? The French didn't believe that George Washington's guerrillas could win the War of Independence without international support, basically from France. One of the main reasons France supported the war was that it didn't want the British to monopolize the opportunity to trade with China." Yet, American revolutionaries, like Franklin, were working with the French against the British Crown while France was attempting to prevent England, a powerful kingdom providing material and financial support to the colonies, from monopolizing trade with China. No wonder King George III called the people behind the American Revolution "traitors."

If there is any doubt that the United States was compromised from the beginning by people who sought to place China in a superior position, consider that a statute of Confucius was erected at the U.S. Supreme Court alongside a statue of Moses. America's founders weren't Chinese – they were English. At the same time, many were Deists.

University of Milan Assistant Professor Giuliano Mori observed, in *Natural Theology and Ancient Theology in the Jesuit-China Mission,* that the Jesuit-China Mission's promotion of Confucianism coincided with the spread of Deism. If Christianity required its followers to accept Jesus as Lord and Savior through faith, Deists recognized Jesus objectively as savior, but only from the perspective of historic knowledge. At the same time, Deists asserted that knowledge of a Supreme Being, or creator of the universe, could be obtained through reason and observation.

The Deist philosophy was almost identical to Confucianism, as promoted and interpreted by the Jesuit-China Mission. If the Papacy originally attempted to claim God's temporal authority through St. Peter, the Jesuits in China attempted to establish China as ruler of the world by claiming that the Chinese prophecies had predicted Jesus. Since China's prophets and philosophers predated Jesus, they were the original purveyors of God's divine truth. However, as would later to be revealed, the Jesuits had simply taken patriarchs from the *Bible* and assigned them Chinese identities, again invalidating their arguments.

French Jesuits "proposed an interpretation of certain characters of the (Confucian canon) as figures of the *Bible*," Mori wrote. "Jesuits generally described the Chinese empire in highly eulogistic terms. The only blemish that could be imputed to the Chinese was intellectual pride, which (they considered) a by-product of their intellectual and moral excellence."

In order to obtain concessions from the Chinese, the Jesuits needed to place China in a superior position – and therefore associate the virtuous qualities of Christian saints and patriarchs with the Chinese and then predate them to identify China as the source of God's divine message. "A form of historical chauvinism had to be taken into account," Mori wrote. "The Chinese would not accept new ideas unless they were proven to derive from ancient and authoritative traditions."

In order to "convert" the Chinese for the purposes of expanding Vatican influence in Central Asia, the Jesuits were tasked with establishing precedents and traditions rooted in Chinese history and interpreting Confucianism through the lens of Christianity. The Jesuit China Mission "did not seek to abolish Confucianism, but rather, perfect it through Christianity," Mori wrote even though from a doctrinal standpoint, Confucianism and Christianity were at odds.

Through "reason," "observation," and rhetoric, the Jesuits thought they could make these connections. They argued that nothing in Confucianism "contained anything that goes against the Catholic faith nor does the Catholic faith impede anything (that relates to Confucianism). On the contrary, it contributes to the tranquility and peace of the republic, which the Confucian books demand."

The republic was based upon Plato's *Republic*, which was then reinterpreted through Confucianism – that peace could only be established if everyone knew and accepted his place within the hierarchy, with humanity enslaved under a class of ruling elite who held a mandate from Heaven to rule over the world. Society was to be regimented, with all aspects of society aligned to serve this divine purpose.

Materialistic at its core, Confucianism was diametrically opposed to Christianity. Through reason and observation, the Deists and Jesuits attempted to make Confucianism superior to Christianity, but consistent with Christian theology. "Confucians believe, like Christians, that there was divine punishment for evil and reward for good," Mori wrote. Names by which Confucians referred to as God, like Tian and Shanghi, literally translate into Heaven and Supreme Deity, and therefore "do not imply anything that was contrary to the true notion of God."

The Jesuits concluded that they could claim "great advantages" by associating Catholicism with Confucianism since the latter was "grounded in natural reason." At the core of Confucianism was Hegelian dialectics – or problem-reaction-solution – that is, that the world's wealth and power could be consolidated within the hands of an elite through perpetual war, revolution, and societal disruption. If the Papacy couldn't pick world rulers, the Jesuits could create conditions that placed leaders into power who secretly served them.

With a view to amassing wealth and power within China, the Jesuits portrayed Confucius as "a great philosopher, possibly even greater than some Greek and Latin thinkers," Mori wrote. "The Christian-like elements in (Confucianism) were hence explainable as the product of a virtuous use of natural reason. This faculty had been given to men as an *alternative route to salvation*, less perfect than revelation, but (consistent with) virtuous paganism."

Yet the interpretations could not be justified by scripture. The Jesuits concluded that "the ancient Chinese had known the true God guided by the light of reason, if nothing else," Mori wrote. "Accordingly, in the eight chapters of the *Tianzhu shiyi*, or *True Meaning of the Lord of Heaven*, the Jesuits enacted a dialogue between a westerner and a Chinese literate. By referring to natural reason and to passages by Confucius, the westerner demonstrates the existence of an omnipotent God, along with many other tenets of the Christian faith, which utterly convince the Chinese scholar."

Since the Chinese could only be convinced of a Supreme deity through pure reason, the Jesuits pursued this strategy, even going so far as to compare Confucius to Plato and Aristotle. By scouring history, they even made the claim that Confucius had prophesied that "the Word (of God) would become flesh," in the form of Jesus, and that this made Confucius a "great philosopher and prophet."

"In order to avoid theological absurdities concerning a Chinese revelation independent from the Judaeo-Christian one, it was necessary to consider Confucius' prophetical knowledge as originating from within the Judaic, and specifically Noahic tradition, thus qualifying Confucius in the tradition outlined by Biblical history," Mori wrote.

As a result of Jesuit efforts to ingratiate themselves with Chinese rulers, the influence of Deists, secularists, and libertines spread throughout Europe in the 17th century, "threatening Catholic and Protestant establishments alike," he observed. "It became clear that the paramount argument used by all sorts of Deists essentially amounted to a naturalistic interpretation of natural theology. Such an interpretation was theologically incorrect, but philosophically revolutionary. It concerned the process through which men could use reason (divine in origin) in order to achieve some knowledge of God through the knowledge of his creation (nature)."

Through reason – and rhetoric – religious orthodoxy could be debunked as preposterous, and morality could be separated from faith, giving the would-be conquerors free rein to do whatever they wished while being entirely morally justified by their actions.

The flawed, self-serving reason of the Jesuits led them to claim that ancient Chinese theologians and leaders, like Fu Xi, the founder of China, descended from Noah, giving rise to Noahide laws that were Confucian in origins and interpretation. They also attempted to demonstrate that China had been founded by Shem "approximately 200 years after the Deluge, when Noah was still alive." Through reason, the Jesuits found "everything good in the wisdom of the pagans" and concluded that Chinese leaders and theology had "originated from Noah and his progeny."

The Jesuits and leaders of the American Revolution, like Ben Franklin, "canonized" Confucius. They believed that "to condemn Confucius was tantamount to condemning natural reason itself," Mori wrote. "According to a somewhat circular argument, the early foundation of China proved and was proven by the fact that China belonged to the tradition of ancient theology. The laws, sciences, and other institutions of the Chinese could not have derived from any other people, but only from the Patriarch Noah, or from his sons and grandsons." The Jesuits also argued that "the Chinese had participated in the revelation of God's law at the hands of Noah's progeny. Not too differently from Judaism, although in a less perfect manner, early Confucianism was a precursor of Christianity and its Christian-like elements were ascribable to the Noahic tradition."

Somehow Confucius had managed to acquire "pristine knowledge of God derived from the Chinese branch of the Noahic tradition." Since Confucius "predicted the coming of Jesus," Confucianism "traced back to the archaic Judaeo-Christian tradition," corrupting both Judaism and Christianity in the process.

The Vatican had never been a true defender of the faith. From the beginning, the Papacy made illegitimate claims – for example, by asserting that a passage in the *Bible* pertaining to St. Peter granted all successive Popes authority to serve as God's temporal power on Earth.

By starting with a false premise and using circular logic and flawed arguments, reason could be used to explain or rationalize anything and make connections that didn't exist. Since the Jesuits and Vatican were principally concerned with amassing the world's wealth and power, how this had to be achieved was not important. In fact, Niccolo Machiavelli's *Prince* was based upon the strategies of a Pope from the de Borgia clan. Machiavelli recommended pursuing power behind a mask of public virtue. If Confucianism provided the means through which the Vatican could claim the authority to rule over others, then the Jesuits would attempt to claim the divine right to rule by asserting that Confucianism predated, preceded, and predicted Jesus and therefore had precedence over those who genuinely held the divine right (rite) to rule. If Chinese Emperors could be convinced that their ancestors were the true patriarchs of the *Bible*, then they could be convinced that they were destined to rule over humanity. Once they had established full control over the Chinese rulers, the Jesuits – and the Vatican, by extension, could claim that authority for itself.

China's ancient history imparted knowledge on the "origin of the world, the creation of the first man and his fall, the Deluge, the Trinity, the notion of human redemption, the angels and the demons, the purgatory, the eternal reward of the just and the punishment of the impious, and other notions."

The story of "rebel angels, the fall of man, the idea of Heaven and redemption, and the notion of Immaculate Conception were all foreshadowed" by the Chinese who "foresaw the eventual advent of Christ," Mori wrote. The ancients confirmed that "thanks to the justice of a single man, the whole universe was brought back to righteousness; the peoples of the whole universe were sustained by the virtue of that man."

The Jesuits employed their "reason" to conclude that "the extraordinary virtues of Christ could not be fully conveyed by a single allegorical figure." Therefore, Chinese theologians had alluded to Christ through a succession of saintlike Chinese Emperors and heroes whose deeds and heroic actions were represented in the person of Jesus and the history of the Messiah.

We have Ben Franklin to bringing Confucianism to the United States. As Wang observed, "Franklin published Confucius' work in America."

To get a sense of how insidious these people were, Wang recounted a story in which veterans from the American Revolution expressed their desire to "hand down their glories, their titles to their descendants, and so they organized the Cinnatus Society for this purpose. Franklin was not happy about the idea of handing down the title, glory to the next generation as that is the inheritance system of aristocratic system of the Europeans which was just what the revolution opposed." If a new Judaeo-Christian establishment formed in America, the revolutionaries would have to stage another revolution to overthrow it.

Passing down an inheritance from parent to child amounts to passing down traditions, values, and wealth from one generation to the next. It is the duty of a parent to protect and support a child and a blessing to pass down traditions through the generations. The *Bible* even commends parents who leave an inheritance for their children. Children shouldn't have to look to the Rothschilds, the Vatican, or the Confucian leaders to define who they are or what they believe nor should they have to depend upon them for their livelihoods.

The elites pass their wealth and titles to their children; at the highest levels, their children are handed high level government, executive, and media positions based upon legacy and genetics alone, even though their qualifications for the appointment are based upon bloodline and nepotism. The aspiring world rulers were not opposed to passing down wealth, traditions, and privileges to their children; they just wanted to retain these privileges for themselves and their bloodlines while preventing others from doing the same.

Franklin recommended that America adopt a Chinese merit system, so that people with talent could be *selected* to serve in the government. Passing the civil service exam in China requires candidates to demonstrate that they have been sufficiently indoctrinated into Confucian ideology before they can assume a government job. In a similar vein, students must parrot whatever ideologies professors require of them before they can receive a passing grade. Without credentials, one cannot advance in one's chosen profession. By controlling who grades the exam, the elite can control who gets appointed.

Rothschild-controlled companies that administer civil service exams have allegedly been caught rigging exams, resulting in class actions that have alleged discrimination against classes of people, like women, who performed well on these tests but were intentionally assigned failing scores, ensuring that the people who were appointed were the people who were selected, not those who necessarily qualified by merit.

Professor Patrick Mendis from the Fairbank Center of Chinese Studies at Harvard University remarked at the 8th World Confucian Conference at Shangri-la Hotel in China that "the confluence of Confucian heritage and Chinese culture had a remarkable influence on America's Founding Fathers. Franklin was America's Confucius. He and other founding leaders of the United States, such as Thomas Paine and Charles Thompson, wrote about Chinese culture, its civilized people, and Confucian ideas."

Franklin brought Paine to the United States to promote *Common Sense,* a pamphlet of nonexistent grievances against the King to provide a pretext for revolution. Paine spoke of revolution for the sake of revolution, consistent with Confucianism, while acknowledging that there was very little support among the colonists for the revolution he was promoting.

"After undergoing the American Revolution and the victorious War of 1812 with their mother country of England, the founding generation of the United States looked to China for inspiration,"

Mendis wrote. "With the Louisiana Purchase from France, President Thomas Jefferson searched for a short-cut to China through the Columbia river-navigation to Seattle for the purpose of commerce."

Alas, the great American experiment was compromised from the beginning. "Through reason and observation, (some of the founders thought they could) find the truth and can arrive at the truth of morals/principles, creating a Humanist morality," Mendis said. "Humans must be guided by their own morality. God should be honored in a way that is most appropriate for the individual and how they can best accomplish this. This includes respecting alternative viewpoints of God."

The Pilgrims fled England to escape religious persecution; they sought to create in North America a society created of, by, and for the free people of God. Religion shapes values. and values shape society. The society they wanted was Judaeo-Christian.

Judaeo-Christianity provides the basis for freedom while Confucianism provides the basis for tyranny. The colonists chose freedom over tyranny. Confucian values were imported through stealth and deception on behalf of self-serving elite who sought to erode the values upon which the nation was founded to provide rational justifications for quest for power. The seeds to the conquest of America were planted by the Founders.

The colonists didn't support human sacrifice, devil worship, or perpetual revolutions, wars, and disruptions, nor were they elitists who sought to consolidate the world's wealth and power into the hands of the few while enslaving the rest. They were egalitarians who wanted the opportunity to live life on their own terms as free, sovereign citizens and in society where justice was blind and elected representatives served the interests of the electorate, not a shadow elite.

After the French and American Revolutions, France and Great Britain were weakened, and the Jesuits, Vatican, and their affiliated merchants solidified their control over these and other countries.

During the Napoleonic Wars, the Holy Roman Empire fell, placing Great Britain, France, and the Vatican into Rothschild debt and therefore under Rothschild control. Through the Napoleonic Wars, the Rothschilds were able to crash the British stock market and acquire breeding rights into the British Royal family, creating an illegitimate

Royal blood line. The dynasty then bred itself into Royal families throughout Europe, creating Manchurian candidates.

During the Napoleonic Wars, Napoleon Bonaparte's brother, Joseph Bonaparte, briefly served as King of Spain, helping to separate the Spanish Monarchy from its colonies. Once the colonies were lost in the Americas, Mexico scooped them up, and then the United States, which was under the influence of the Vatican, claimed the territory for itself. The Vatican, by this point, was controlled by Rothschild.

Through each successive generation, each war, each revolution, wealth and power was consolidated into fewer hands – and leaders became more corrupt and tyrannical. Dictators emerged during the first half of the 20th century who ruled as if holding a mandate from Heaven. German Fuhrer Adolf Hitler and Soviet Premier Joseph Stalin, both Rothschild bloodlines, ruled in the mold of Central Asian warlords; they purged dissenters, embarked upon homicidal rampages, absconded with wealth, and consolidate industry and natural resources under corporate chieftains.

Most people have heard of the French Revolution, American Revolution, Chinese Revolution, Russian Revolution, possibly even the revolutions of 1848, but has anyone heard of the Mongolian Revolution? The Rothschilds are nothing, if not predictable.

Mongolian Purge

A nineteenth century imperial geographer and explorer of Central and East Asia by the name of Nikolay Mikhaylovich Przhevalsky wrote, "You can penetrate anywhere (in Central Asia), only not with the Gospels under your arm, but with money in your pocket, a carbine in one hand and a whip in the other. Europeans must use these to come and bear away in the name of civilization all these dregs of the human race. A thousand of our soldiers would be enough to subdue all of Asia from Lake Baykal to the Himalayas. Here the exploits of Cortez can still be repeated."

The leaders of Central Asia were "nothing more than political impostors," Przhevalsky said. Central Asians are "constantly cursing their governments and expressing their desire to become Russian subjects. The savage Asiatic clearly understands Russia power is the guarantee for prosperity."

These were the words of a man who was alleged to have been the biological father of Soviet Premier Joseph Stalin. Not only does Przhevalsky physically resembles the dictator, but during Stalin's reign of terror, Przhevalsky's works were promoted throughout the Soviet Union.

Nikolsy Mikhaylovich Przhevalsky
(credit: Britannica)

Joseph Stalin
(credit: IBT Times)

Stalin was born in Tbilisi, Georgia, which served as a trading post for Mongolians and other meandering Central Asian tribes. These were the tribes from which the Bolsheviks were recruited. They were blood-thirsty, ruthless, psychopathic order followers who rejected God for the pursuit of wealth and power through terror. Drawing inspiration from Marxism (and Confucianism), the Bolsheviks rampaged through the streets of Russia, slaughtering innocents, burning down homes, and stealing whatever they could get their hands on.

Stalin was a humble worker who became radicalized while employed at a Rothschild business in Georgia. According to an 1881 ledger, money was secretly transferred to Stalin's mother from a mysterious source around the time of Stalin's birth, reflecting a pattern consistent with Rothschild bastard children who are placed in obscure families and given the financial and professional they need for the historic role they will serve to do the most good for the Rothschilds.

If Przhevalsky were Stalin's actual biological father, this connection helps establish the Rothschilds' origins in Central Asia. Among Przhevalsky's partners was Pyotr Kuzmich Kozlov, whom

Przhevalsky mentored before embarking on trips to Tibet and Mongolia. While researching the Qing dynasty in 1905, Kozlov reported that the British War Office received quite the "fright" after the Dalai Lama expressed his intention to "settle within the confines of Russia."

By this time, the Qing Emperor had established his authority over the Dalai Lama and was unleashing horde armies against targeted rulers and countries. The hordes were ruthless to the kill and skilled at warfare. England was already under the control of the Rothschilds, with few truly grasping why British foreign policy had become so militant and imperialistic. Christians among the British ruling classes had forged alliances with the Christian rulers of Russia while the Rothschilds and Vatican were undermining both.

The English were a civilized, compassionate, if paternalistic, people who nurtured and protected those under their charge. They generously invested in their subjects, built schools, churches, and governmental institutions, helping their people develop the skills and acquire the technologies they needed to improve their societies and lives. The British respected the traditions of the disparate people of their empire and sought to build mutually beneficial relationships. Even if the British pursued resources, like oil, from countries they had conquered, they reinvested in those countries, helping to elevate the standard of living, promote human rights, and establish common law courts and responsible, democratic governments for the people. The English produced William Shakespeare and had attempted to create a society of, by, and for a free, God-fearing people in North America. The spirit of God lived within the hearts, minds, and souls of the British people.

In contrast, the British Empire under Rothschild pursued gunboat diplomacy and militant imperialism in which people were enslaved, trafficked, and exterminated. The relationships forged under Rothschild were one-sided – that is, resources were extracted principally to enrich the dynasty and its affiliated interests while people, societies, and traditions were treated with contempt and callous disregard. Once they controlled the British Monarchy, the Rothschilds promoted an agenda for a global dystopia depicted in Aldous Huxley's *Brave New World* and George Orwell's *1984,* much to the disgust of the British. The future the dynasty envisioned was one of a proverbial boot kicking the face of humanity for all eternity.

As revolution and war raged through Eurasia in the early part of the 20th century, a little mentioned Mongolian Revolution was launched to purge the Mongolians with money, power, and influence.

The Mongolian People's Republic was led by Khorlooglin Choibalsan, the Marshall of the Mongolian People's Army from 1930. Choibalsan died the same year as Stalin – in 1952, ensuring that he didn't publicize the details of his alliance with the blood-thirsty Soviet dictator.

As the "Stalin of Mongolia," Choibalsan engaged in Soviet-style purges that resulted in the deaths of between 30,000 to 35,000 Mongolians. Among the purged were Buddhist clergy, the intelligentsia, political dissidents, and other other "enemies of the revolution."

Choibalsan was trained and radicalized in Russia. He was then recruited to join the revolutionary Consular Hill group, which resisted Chinese occupation in Outer Mongolia after 1919.

If the Rothschilds effectively controlled the Qing dynasty and the Soviet Union, what was the point of promoting revolution in Mongolia? To consolidate power and wealth under centralized control. First, power was centralized in the Soviet Union under a Rothschild bloodline. Once this had been accomplished, a Chinese Communist Revolution, led by Rothschild bloodline Chairman Mao Tse-tung, consolidated power further in China.

Following the revolution in Mongolia, a Mongolian republic was established with Rothschild puppet leaders running the government to ensure that the country was stable and conducive to business and that its resources could be commandeered for Rothschild use.

Among the members of the Mongolian revolutionary leadership were Dambyn Chagdarjay, Darizavy Losol -- and Dogsomyn Bodoo, who was Choibalsan's teacher at the Russian-Monoglian school for translators and a spitting image of Russian President Vladimir Putin.

As founding member of the Mongolian People's Revolutionary Party, Bodoo was elected leader of Mongolia's provisional government. After the Outer Mongolian Revolution, Bodoo became first Mongolian Prime Minister. Following the pattern of other Communist puppet regimes, Mongolia established a secret anti-

Chinese resistance and revolutionary organization.

The White Army, which represented the Russian Romanovs and Christian aristocrats, attempted to protect the Mongolians from Stalin's purge. To this end, an anti-Bolshevik Russian warlord and baron in the Tsarist service by the name of Roman von Ungern-Sternberg invaded Mongolia and pushed back the Red (Bolshevik) Army. As commander of an offshoot of the White Army in the Far East, the baron occupied Outer Mongolia in 1921, leading the Bogy Khan to name him Khan of Mongolia. Von Ungern-Sternberg was able to provide the financial and material support the Mongolians needed to independence, but China refused to recognize the new government. As a reward for his efforts, Stalin's Red Army hunted him down and executed him.

As the revolution raged on, Choibalsan became Deputy Chief of the Mongolian People's Army and Chairman of the Mongolian Revolutionary Youth League. Bodoo was eventually purged and executed while Choibalsan was stripped of his party membership and position as deputy commander of Mongolian military. After Choibalsan had outlived his usefulness, his political influence dwindled.

Mongolia then entered a period of Right Opportunism, based upon Lenin's New Economic Policy in the Soviet Union. As Stalin increased his power, Mongolia entered a "leftist period" at which point Choibalsan was "kicked upstairs" to serve as head of state to implement Soviet policies for rapid collectivization, land seizures, and the persecution of Buddhists.

During the period of Right Opportunism, Mongolian herders were forced off their land to make way for poorly managed collective farms that slaughtered one-third of the livestock.

The property and treasures of Mongolian nobles and Buddhist priests were then seized. The Communists executed them in a manner eerily reminiscent of the French Revolution, reflecting that the rational Enlightenment-inspired revolutions were not about promoting democratic ideals but advancing an agenda for tyranny and plunder.

While onlookers recoiled in horror over the barbarism of the Communists, a "cult of personality" was built around Choibalsan to portray him as a kindly moderate who sought to curtail the excesses of the revolution even though he was a key player in the bloodshed and revolution. The Mongolian purges mirrored the Stalin purges almost to the letter. While Stalin ordered the extermination of Jews, Choibalsan executed Buddhists and targeted dissidents through show trials, executions, torture, and forced labor. Anyone who challenged what he had done or attempted to sabotage Mongolia-Soviet relations was promptly executed.

Another Great Terror was then launched to put down counter revolutionary activity. In this next purge, twenty-three high ranking lamas were arrested and executed. Anyone who dared protest the executions was arrested and shot on the spot.

Mongolia's resources were then commandeered to fuel the Soviet war machine. Mongolia increased its livestock population to provide the Soviet Union with raw materials in preparation for war against Europe. In other words, Rothschild puppet leaders ensured that resources intended for the people were used to support the dynasty's relentless quest for empire. Mongolia's food, military clothing, sheepskin, boots, fur coats, financial resources were seized from Mongolia and reallocated to support Soviet military units. Choibalsan even traveled to Moscow to pass out gifts to the Red Army. Afterward, Stalin conferred upon him the Order of Lenin for his outstanding service.

After consolidating power, Choibalsan became Mongolia's supreme leader, allowing him to hold the offices of Prime Minister, Minister for Internal Affairs, Minister of War, and Commander in Chief of the Mongolian Armed Forces simultaneously.

In 1940, Choibalsan purged his Secretary General and replaced him with Stalin's preferred candidate. Once he entered retirement, Choibalsan continued to align Mongolian and Soviet policy. He then rewrote the Mongolian Constitution to crush the power of the Buddhist priests, using the Soviet Constitution as a template.

Once threats to his power were eliminated, Choibalsan pursued a "Greater Mongolia." To this end, he unified Outer and Inner Mongolia, promoted socialism, and "exterminated the concept of property."

After the revolution, the Mongolian government launched a Five Year Plan (1948-1952) for modernization, with Soviet funding. Modeled after a similar Soviet plan, the Mongolians pursued economic development, invested in infrastructure and energy grids, and restocked the country's livestock.

In the ensuing years, Mongolia deepened its economic, political, and diplomatic ties with the Soviet Union and established diplomatic relations with North Korea and later, the People's Republic of China (PRC), all Rothschild puppet regimes. Mongolia became the first country to recognize the PRC. Predictably, all Soviet satellite countries established formal diplomatic ties with Mongolia. In 2017, the Mongolian Bank celebrated Choibalsan's bloody legacy by minting a coin with his image.

Communist Double Speak

The history of Tartaria, as Central Asia has historically been known, was buried after World War II, no doubt as the truth would have exposed the origins of the darkness overtaking the world, possibly derailing Rothschild's quest for world domination. As the philosopher George Santayana reminds us, those who do not remember history are doomed to repeat it, and so the Rothschilds ensured that the public did not know history. If Rothschild controlled the governments, and schools relied upon the government for funding, then the dynasty's preferred academics could provide a whitewashed versions of history that they wanted the public to believe.

A CIA document created in 1957 that was declassified in 1998 provides a glimpse into the relationship between the Tartars and the Soviet Union. Based upon this document, on August 9, 1944, the Central Committee of the Communist party in Moscow issued a directive ordering the party's Tartar Provincial Committee "to proceed to a scientific revision of the history of Tartaria, to liquidate serious shortcomings and mistakes of a nationalistic character committed by individual writers and historians in dealing with Tartar history."

In other words, historians were instructed to rewrite the history of the Tartars to put the Soviet Union (USSR) in a good light. At the time, the USSR was controlled by the Rothschilds through Stalin and numerous other political, military, and economic links.

Since then, Tartaria has been eliminated from history books and maps. If the truth of the Tartars were known, the Rothschilds would no longer be able to portray themselves as savvy bankers and aristocrats, the noble advisors to governments and Monarchs, generous patrons of the arts and philanthropists who loved and supported the Jewish people, or as benevolent overlords who are attempting to elevate the moral climate of the world with the Vatican, and empower disparate people throughout the world.

If one were to look into the dynasty's rise to power, one would see that they have sacrificed hundreds of millions of people, perhaps billions, in their quest for empire. The ancestors, relatives, and friends of all of us have been sacrificed to the cause – and along with them, their traditions, hopes, dreams, wealth, all sacrificed to feed the psychopathic narcissism of these truly deranged people. Their evil was so great that they had to control narratives, manage the media, rewrite history, compromise political and corporate leaders, threaten, intimidate, and assassinate people to keep the truth from being known. They were absolutely terrified of the truth, so let's give it to them.

On August 24, 1999, the CIA released a paper entitled *National Cultural Development under Communism,* which reveals the treachery of the Communists. In a proclamation issued on December 7 1917 over the signature of Lenin and Stalin, which was addressed to "All Muslims toilers of Russia and the East," the Bolsheviks stated: "Muslims of Russia, Tartars of the Volga, and the Crimea, and Turkestan, Turks and Tartars of Transcaucasia, Chechens and Mountain People of the Caucasus, and all you whose mosques and prayer houses have been destroyed, whose beliefs and customs have been trampled upon by the Tsars and the oppressors of Russia. Henceforth your beliefs and customs, your national and cultural institutions are forever free and inviolate. Organize your national life in complete freedom. This is your right."

In this document, the CIA explains why the appeal was written in this way: "The Bolsheviks had realized that if their revolution was to be a complete success, and if they were to be able to consolidate their newly won power, the support of Russia's minority peoples, including the Muslims, was essential. The Muslim peoples of Russia had, at the time, no way of knowing how little a Bolshevik (Communist) promise meant."

The Muslims had become colonial subjects of the Tsar who did not violate their rights, but treated the Muslims extremely well, despite wounding Muslim pride by incorporating their territory into the

Russian empire.

The Communists pursued identity politics and jingoism, as is their practice, to mobilize the Muslims against the Russian Royal family while the Bolsheviks planned the purge. The Communist invitation "to declare (your) freedom from Russian rule and create (your) own national states initially appealed to the Muslims, and so the "(Muslims) were easily persuaded to cooperate with the (Bolsheviks)," the CIA reported.

The Russian revolutionary, Vladimir Lenin, said that "Everyone must be perfectly free not only to belong to whatever religion he pleases, but he must be free to disseminate his religion and to change his religion." Does this not sound eerily familiar to the leaders of the American Revolution who sought "freedom of religion," only to have elites turn around and try to suppress Christianity through the World Council of Church, community organizers, and radical activist groups? The newly minted elite wanted the freedom to "do as thou wilt," to engage in religious practices that mainstream religions rejected.

"No official should be entitled to ask anyone about his religion. It is a matter for that person's conscience and no one has any business to interfere," Lenin continued as if spouting rational Enlightenment talking points. The globalists wanted the freedom to be as evil as their dark hearts compelled them. The only religion the Communists sought to protect was their own.

Once the Communists inspired the confidence of the Muslims, they ruthlessly suppressed Islam. In November of 1917, the Muslims were told that they were free to "continue in the practice of their faith." However, once the Communists had consolidated their power, their mask slipped, revealing that they had no intention of honoring their promises. Mosques were confiscated and shut down; Muslim brotherhoods, outlawed; and a campaign was launched to ridicule Islam and its spiritual leaders. Stalin frequently vilified Muslim, Tartar, and Buddhist cultural heroes before liquidating their respective communities.

When the Communists came to power in 1917, there were 7,000 mosques in Russia and many thousands more in Muslim Central Asia, the Caucasus and Transcaucasia, and the Crimea. By 1942, there were only 1,321 mosques in the USSR, with many confiscated and converted into warehouses. "Political expediency required the

Communists to make promises now and break them later," the CIA reported.

For a while, Stalin praised Sharia law, which was described in the Soviet political dictionary as a "means for keeping the workers in economic and political subordination by the rich. It legalizes domination, exploitation, and slavery of the workers, and enslavement of women."

During the purge, religious institutions were destroyed; language was corrupted; rights were curtailed; and the ability of people to govern themselves was restricted.

The CIA concluded: "(Before) (the Muslims) were subject colonial peoples of Tsarist Russia; today they are subject colonial peoples of Soviet Russia. The only difference is that under Tsarist rule, they enjoyed cultural autonomy, whereas today despite the Communist boast of free cultural development permitted every nation within the borders of Russia, cultures and rights are being curtailed by the needs of greater Russian chauvinism. (Other) Muslim peoples of the world would do well to reflect on the fate of their unfortunate coreligionists before they accept the Communist propaganda now being directed at them. For there can be little doubt that if ever the Communists were to gain control of their lands, they would suffer the same fate."

Normalizing The Abnormal

The National Committee of U.S.-China Relations was established in 1966 to help neutralize America's resistance to Communist China through a process of reeducation and indoctrination. Professors, legislators, journalists, business executives, and other people of influence were enlisted to promote a positive image of China to address the public's skepticism and concerns about opening doors to this country.

As the public's resistance to China softened, President Richard Nixon and his Secretary of State, Henry Kissinger, who had been trained in London for this role, normalized relations with China. The Secretary of State engaged Chairman Mao Tse-tung to move the agenda forward through diplomatic channels. Ambitious presidential aspirants, like Sen. Ted Kennedy and Sen. John Edwards, were all too willing to advance China's agenda over the interests of the United

States in order to receive the establishment's support for their respective political campaigns. Kissinger assumed leadership in opening up channels for technology transfers to Israel, China, and other countries, some of which were rivals to the United States, transforming America's military into a military shop. That this was done should not come as a surprise, considering that the merchant classes had always relied upon the military to protect their markets.

The agenda gained momentum during the Clinton Administration. While campaigning for the presidency, Bill Clinton, a Rothschild bloodline, received substantial financial support from Communist China. He was not the preferred candidate for the nomination as scandals dogged him in Little Rock, Arkansas. Moreover, his wife, Hillary Clinton, worked at the Rose Law firm where she had allegedly stolen patents and acquired back door key access into computer systems. Both were Yale graduates who threw caution to the wind to implement the Rothschild globalist agenda.

After receiving generous campaign contributions from Communist China, President Clinton appointed Communist Chinese officials to sensitive trade missions, compromising national security in the process. As concerned patriots on Capitol Hill raised the alarm about China, Congressman Tom DcLay and House Speaker Newt Gingrich intervened to redirect the public's attention to allegations concerning the president's sexual misconduct. The Lewinsky scandal was then pursued by independent counsel Ken Starr, the nephew of C.V. Starr who had laid the foundation for the transfer of America's manufacturing base to China prior to World War II.

Both Republicans and Democrats, whose political campaigns relied upon corporate money, were all too willing to do China's bidding on behalf of corporate America which sought to tap China's lucrative markets. Accommodating these interests set the stage for America's jobs and manufacturing base to be shipped overseas.

The Clintons were eager to move full steam ahead with the technocratic agenda – that of identifying, tracking, and tracing all American citizens so that they could be more effectively managed and surveiled through technology. Patriots within the federal government clearly understood the agenda at play. While elites opened up the Internet to track, trace, and create files on each citizen, patriots were creating and maintaining files on the elite, essentially using the weapons the elite had created to enslave humanity to entrap the elite.

Others, like Edward Snowden, alerted the public to the emerging surveillance state that was infringing upon the public's privacy under the cover of fighting the "war on terrorism."

While President Clinton mobilized Democrats behind China's entry into the World Trade Organization, DeLay and Gingrich worked on securing Republican support for China. At the same time, any corporations seeking to do business in China were required to pass along their trade secrets to the Communist Chinese government before they were allowed access to its coveted markets. There were even reports of Chinese nationals sitting in the U.S. Patent and Trademark Office copying patents as soon as they were submitted and then passing the patents along to China to produce products cheaply and ahead of the Americans, thereby, preventing American inventors from being able to capitalize on their own inventions.

Former Federal Reserve Chairman Alan Greenspan was present at the creation of the Internet. During the Clinton Administration, "we had debates about the Internet's potential," he wrote in his autobiography. The dot.com boom and technocracy were born on August 5, 1995 in Silicon Valley with the launch of the Netscape Internet browser.

Silicon-based electronics and micro-systems technology drove the tech boom. The Internet of Things and singularity followed soon after. Computer chips, which relied upon silicon for semiconductor electronics and transistors, gave birth to a number of new technologies, including cell phones, genetic engineering microprocessors, lasers, disk drives, video tape, computer games, and computers.

Northern California was chosen for the Silicon launch given the Jesuit ties to this state. Establishing Vatican roots here, Spanish priest Junipero Serra erected missions throughout California, starting with San Diego. The missions became a focal point and driver of economic activity in the state.

In 1846, during the Mexican-American War, the port of San Francisco was conquered by the U.S. Army, allowing the military to take possession of all of northern California. U.S. President James Polk, in his capacity as constitutional commander-in-chief of the Army and Navy, authorized the military and naval commanders of the United States in California to exercise the belligerent rights of a conqueror to form a civil and military government for the purposes of imposing duties on imports.

The man who was credited with "conquering" California was Colonel Richard Barnes Mason, who became the fifth military governor of California before statehood was achieved. A bloodline, Mason was a direct descendant of George Mason, a Founding Father who helped draft the U.S. Constitution and Bill of Rights. "The recent instructions from the President of the United States made the officers of the Army and Navy the collectors of customs in California," Mason said, establishing control over California's ports.

Once the treaty of peace was signed between the United States and Mexico in 1848, Jesuits established institutions of higher learning throughout the state, strengthening the Vatican's influence here. Mason went on to draft the official report that spurred California's gold rush attracting people to the state, like Leland Stanford, an industrialist from New York who founded Stanford University. Stanford later became California governor. Wherever the Vatican established its roots, it pushed the China-Rothschild agenda. To get a sense of where the Vatican and Rothschilds wish to take the United States, just look at California, with its tent cities, punishing taxes, draconian laws, rampant crime, cultural Marxism, societal decay, high gas prices, and radical politicians who champion the interests of the Vatican.

IV.
Greenspan's Enlightenment

Alan Greenspan, who served as 13th Chairman of the Federal Reserve from 1987 to 2006, was sold hook, line, and sinker on the rational Enlightenment after canoodling with the financial elite. As an economics student at New York University, Greenspan worked under Eugene Banks, the managing director of Brown Brothers Harriman (BBH), toiling away in the equity department of one of the largest private investment firms in the United States that just happens to cater to high net worth individuals. The firm reportedly manages some $3.3 trillion in assets and has employed such pillars of the establishment as W. Averell Harriman and Prescott Bush, whose bloodline produced two Presidents.

A legend in his own right, Harriman was among the founders of Brown Brothers. His career was launched in the linen mercantile trading business, reflecting the lasting influence of the Hanseatic League and its powerful commercial ties to China. Harriman graduated from Yale, the university that groomed Mao Tse-tung, and partnered with industrialists who bankrolled Adolf Hitler and the Nazis.

During World War II, Harriman facilitated communication between Prime Minister Winston Churchill and Franklin Delano Roosevelt (FDR), helping to draw the United States into a war to support Britain (Rothschild)'s imperialist designs. The war was transformative, helping to reorganize Europe under Rothschild control, starting with the European Coal and Steel Community, a foundational next step towards the European Union which eventually gave rise to global institutions like the United Nations in which Rothschild bloodline Joseph Stalin was given a seat, allowing him access to American military strategies that ensured the United States would never win another war.

The debt created by the World Wars provided the pretext for an income tax, which became permanent, allowing elites to dip into the pockets of hard working Americans to subsidize their schemes.

After the Second World War, FDR, Churchill, and Stalin decided at Yalta to commit their respective countries to elevating Communist China to leader of the New World Order while reducing the United States to a bankrupt welfare state.

Greenspan was a malleable, eager student who found himself surrounded by the ruling elite and inspired by their globalist plans. His career would reach into the stratosphere of success as long as he towed the line.

After joining the firm, Greenspan's career took off, allowing him to walk through doors that the banker, as a poor boy from Brooklyn, couldn't even imagine.

Soon the banker found himself rubbing shoulders with celebrities, dating famous television journalists, and the first in line for consideration for coveted appointments. All he had to do was tow the line in service of the agenda and all doors would magically open before him. Among the glitterati who moved in Greenspan's circles were the objectivist Ayn Rand, Brooke Astor, Henry Kissinger, David Rockefeller, and ABC News superstar Barbara Walters. He met Walters at a party hosted by Nelson Rockefeller in Washington, DC and began dating her.

In 1948, Greenspan worked as analyst for the National Industrial Conference Board, a business and industry oriented think tank in New York. Seven years later, he became Chairman of the Federal Reserve, a position he held for three decades.

Throughout his career, Greenspan championed the rational Enlightenment. He loved President Ronald Reagan's deregulation, "which implies much less government support for the downtrodden," he said. "Mainstream Republicans were conflicted about thinking or talking in such terms because they seemed contrary to Judaeo-Christian values. Not Reagan. It's not that there wasn't sympathy for people who, through not fault of their own find themselves in dire straits, but that wasn't government's role."

Yet, it was the government's role to bail out Big Business time and time again. "Tough love in the long run is love," Greenspan said.

After a meeting of minds, Reagan made Greenspan Chairman of the Federal Reserve Board. The banker then joined a number of corporations as director, including, for example, Capitol Cities/ABC, JP Morgan Chase, and Mobil. Between 1982 and 1988, Greenspan was tapped to serve as Director of the Council on Foreign Affairs, a sister think tank to the London-based Royal Institute of International Affairs, which promotes foreign policy that supports Rothschild's larger imperialist designs.

In 1984, Greenspan was appointed to the board of the Group of Thirty (G-30), which was established in 1978 at the initiative of the Rockefeller Foundation as a council of private and central bankers. The first G-30 Chairman was Johannes Wittleveen, a former director of the International Monetary Fund; its founder was Geoffrey Bell, who worked for Schroders, which was founded by a Hanseatic family who issued bonds for the Confederacy during the Civil War.

Bell, in turn, was assistant to Gordon Richardson, the Governor of the Bank of England who was employed in Her Majesty's Treasury and who served as Chairman of the Pilgrims Trust, which was founded by a partner of a Standard Oil affiliate. In addition to serving on the Queen's Privy Council, Richardson donated generously to Yale University. Curiously, Richardson patronized the Metropolitan Museum of Art in New York. The Met acquired the Temple of Dendur which was commissioned by Caesar Augustus and dedicated to Isis, Osiris, and Horus.

President George H.W. Bush renewed Greenspan's appointment at the Federal Reserve only to blame him for the sluggish economy that contributed to his one-term presidency. Greenspan thought this accusation unfair, though he was delighted to be assigned to a seat next to Hillary Clinton at President Bill Clinton's inauguration. "I assumed that my invitation to sit with the First Lady was a matter of courtesy," he said. "Mrs. Clinton was wearing a bright red suit, and as the President spoke, the cameras focused on us again and again."

He met with the Clinton Transition team in Little Rock, Arkansas to help staff the new Administration which pushed through free trade. "Clinton impressed me by fighting for the ratification of (the North American Free Trade Agreement),," Greenspan said. "The treaty negotiated under President Bush was designed to phase out tariffs and other trade barriers between Mexico and the United States, though it also included Canada. Labor unions hated it, and so did most Democrats as well as some conservatives. Few Congress watchers thought it had a prayer. But Clinton argued, in effect, that you cannot stop the world from turning, like it or not. America was increasingly part of the international economy, and NAFTA embodied the belief that trade and competition create prosperity, and you need free markets to do that. He and the White House staff went all out, and after a two month struggle, they got the treaty approved."

When Americans began to lose their jobs to cheap labor overseas, Greenspan suggested that displaced workers receive unemployment insurance. At the same time, he supported H-IB visa programs, which forced American workers to train their foreign replacements, who were willing to work for less, boosting corporate profits.

During the second Bush Administration, Greenspan recommended that President George W. Bush depose Iraqi leader Saddam Hussein to keep oil prices low to prevent the global economy from falling into chaos and bringing the industrial world "to its knees." That it was even possible for the industrial world to be brought to its knees by a foreign country's curtailment of oil was a direct consequence of policies laid out during the Nixon Administration on behalf of Rothschild. After oil was discovered in Prudhoe Bay, Alaska, the United States was on path to becoming energy independence as enough oil had been discovered to last hundreds of years, Pastor Lindsey Williams observed in *The Non-Energy Crisis.* Kissinger prevented the oil from being tapped so that America would be dependent upon foreign oil and easier to manipulate and subdue.

In the wake of the subprime mortgage crisis of 2008 that resulted in mass foreclosures and job losses throughout the United States, Greenspan was forced to account for the policies he had set in motion. As *The New York Times* reported, "a humbled Mr. Greenspan admitted that he had put too much faith in the self-correcting power of free markets. Mr. Greenspan refused to accept blame for the crisis, but acknowledged that his belief in deregulation had been shaken."

"You found your view of the world, your ideology, was not right, it was not working," Congressman Henry Waxman asked Greenspan in hearings.

"Absolutely, precisely," Greenspan replied. "You know, that's precisely the reason I was shocked, because I have been going more than 40 years or more with very considerable evidence that it was working considerably well."

What went wrong?

"Infectious greed."

As Greenspan explained: "I explored critical elements of this emerging global environment: the principles of governing it that arose out of the Enlightenment of the eighteenth century, the vast energy infrastructure that powers it, the global financial imbalances, and the dramatic shifts in world demographics that threaten it, and despite its unquestioned success, the chronic concern over the justice of the distribution of its rewards. Finally I bring together what we can reasonably conjecture about the makeup of the world economy in 2030."

Greenspan had exposed himself to be a puppet and parrot of an agenda whose religion was simply profits and power at any cost.

We, the people were not to be considered in the calculations. As journalist Matt Taibbi reported, bankers like Greenspan reinforced a system that was rigged on behalf of the elite: "Every time the banks blew up a speculative bubble, they could go back to the Fed and borrow money at zero or one or two percent, and then start the game all over," making it "almost impossible" for the banks to lose money. According to Taibbi, Greenspan was a "classic conman (who) flattered and bullshitted his way up the Matterhorn of American power and jacked himself off to the attention of Wall Street for 20 consecutive years."

Even though he was merely an order taker, Greenspan was scapegoated for the disastrous policies he had set in motion. *Time* described him as one of the "twenty-five people to blame for the financial crisis." Of course, the news magazine did not assign blame where it belonged – to the elites behind the curtain.

The subprime mortgage crisis was born in Rothschild and Vatican-controlled Indian Country to help Indians acquire loans for homes they might not have qualified for based upon income, with the contingency that the federal government would bail out either the tribes or the banks in case the tribal member defaulted. Reducing people to dependency and then spearheading programs to care for them, while serving as intermediary to receive a tremendous cut, was big business and one which exploited those most in need to enrich those who already had more than they could ever hope to want. Such policies were in the "rational self interest" of those who promoted them, evidenced by the profits made.

Greenspan's book, *The Age of Turbulence*, was enormously prescient. After September 11, 2001, Greenspan wrote: "The Federal Reserve is in charge of the electronic payment systems that transfer more than four trillion dollars a day in money and securities between banks all over the country and the rest of the world. We always thought that if you wanted to cripple the U.S. economy, you'd take out the payment systems."

Two decades later, financial leaders are promoting electronic payment systems that could be hacked by malicious third parties, some of them foreign actors, with bitcoin promoted as the solution to emerging global financial problems. Overnight, people who had amassed a fortune in bitcoin found themselves locked out of their own electronic wallets with no way to access the money.

Greenspan anticipated future shocks to the economy that would lead people to appreciate the value of working remotely in the interests of efficiency: "A shock like the one we'd just sustained (after September 11, 2001) could lead to a massive withdraw from and major contraction in economic activity," he wrote. "The misery could multiply," thus justifying more bailouts for Big Business.

Thanks to data collection efforts, bankers can anticipate how the markets will respond to different conditions: "The Federal Reserve system consists of twelve banks strategically situated around the country. Each one lends money to and regulates the banks in its region. The Federal Reserve bank officers and staff stay constantly in touch with bankers and business people in their districts. Information they glean about orders and sales beats official published data by as much as a month." Information was being collected through analytics made possibly by such companies as Google and Facebook that grew out of the technocracy the Clintons had spawned in anticipation of this inevitability.

The elites wanted to know as much as they could about consumer choices so that they could regulate those choices and determine how much money was being spent, where, and by whom. More importantly, they wanted to know how shocks would impact consumer choices and individual lives. "People appear motivated by the inbred striving for self- esteem that is, in large part, fostered by the approval of others," Greenspan said. "This induces people to work in plants and offices side-by-side even though they will soon have the technical capability of contributing in isolation through cyberspace."

Among the obstacles that globalists will have to overcome, he said, are "nativism, tribalism, populism, indeed all of the isms into which communities retreat when their identities are under siege," he said.

In the face of growing criticism over the destructiveness of his policies, Greenspan admitted that he was just "an implementer of orders rather than a leader."

During the Clinton Administration, Greenspan had the opportunity to promote China's entry into the WTO and Bank of International Settlements so that Communist China, one of the biggest threats to freedom on the planet, could coordinate global financial policy with other bankers. "China's central bankers now play a key role in the Bank of International Settlements in Switzerland, an institution long associated with capitalist international finance," he said. "Just a few years removed from isolated central planning, (the Chinese) have become major players in operating the global financial system." Thanks to Greenspan, all central bankers are "working together for a single goal," he said. "Strategies come and go, but the ultimate competitive goal remains gaining the maximum rate of return, adjusted for risk. Competition efficiently works, whatever the strategy, provided free and open markets prevail."

The Queen's Loyal Subject

In 2002, Greenspan was knighted by Queen Elizabeth II for his contribution to global stability. The banker's wife, NBC-TV correspondent Andrea Mitchell, accompanied him to the Royal family's Balmoral estate in the Scottish Highlands where he joked with the Queen and her husband, Prince Philip, "The British Government put me to work yesterday."

Greenspan clarified at a keynote speech in London held on September 25, 2002 at the HM Treasury Building that "I am daily reminded of the special relationship the Federal Reserve has had over the decades with decision makers from the British government. Literally twenty feet from my desk are plaques commemorating the numerous World War II meetings in our Board Room between the combined military chiefs of the United States and Great Britain that set the pattern for Allied collaboration and the successful prosecution of World War II."

The ties between the Bank of England and the Federal Reserve were cemented in the 1920s through the relationship of Benjamin Strong, the President of the New York Federal Reserve Bank; and Baron Montague Norman, the Governor of the Bank of England.

Known as "the currency dictator of Europe," Norman was god father to the children of Hitler's President of the Reichsbank and Minister of Economic Affairs -- and a member of the Bank of International Settlements (BIS), the world bank for the central banks. According to BIS records, Norman put Britain on the gold standard and then transferred that gold to the Nazi regime. Recognized as Grand Officer of the Order of the Crown, he also served on the Queen's Privy Council.

A key player in shaping global financial policy, Norman was reportedly the only man in history whose maternal grandfather and paternal grandfather both served as Governor of the Bank of England. His father worked for the London branch of Brown Brothers.

"To us at the Federal Reserve, the Bank of England projects a nearly mythical presence as the developer of much of the central banking we all practice today," Greenspan said. "The Federal Reserve's close relationship with the Bank of England and other major central banks has been enhanced through periodic meetings at the (BIS) in Basel since 1963. (There are) regular meetings of the finance ministers and central bankers of the Group of Five (G-5), and later the Group of Seven (G-7), that interactions between the Federal Reserve and the British Treasury and other major finance ministries have taken of special importance."

Among the organizations that oversaw the meetings was the Organization of Economic Cooperation and Development (OECD), which has been monitoring consumer spending habits around the world for the purposes of coordinating economic activity on a global scale to maximize profits and drive consumer spending. "We all participate in the deliberation of the IMF and the World Bank," Greenspan said. "But the G-7 has surfaced as the most significant forum through which both finance ministers and central bankers from the major countries coordinate on economic issues."

Back to The Lagoon

The lagoons of Venice could be seen as the source of the trouble now confronting Western Civilization. The merchants of Venice were among the explorers who journeyed into Central Asia where they partnered with blood-thirsty mercenaries to expand and protect their markets, eventually making their way into the Hanseatic League and East India Company, transforming what should have been a benevolent commercial enterprise into a destructive imperialist force.

It should come as no surprise that Greenspan, whose career has been dedicated to implementing the agenda pursued by global financial planners, would one day make his way back to Venice, where he rediscovered his humanity.

In Venice, Greenspan appears to have gleaned some insight into the stupidity and destructiveness of the ideas he has been promoting his entire life, that of an unrestrained push for profits, efficiency, and creative destruction on behalf of corporations without considering the impact on humanity, the nation, or whether the improvements he sought were even needed. Progress for the sake of progress has destroyed America at its foundation, but it made Greenspan exceedingly rich and so it served his "rational self interest."

After visiting the Italian lagoon with Andrea Mitchell, Greenspan remarked:

As necessary as creative destruction is to the material standards of living, it's no coincidence that some of the world's most cherished places are those that have changed the least over the centuries.

I'd never visited the city, and like so many travelers before me, I was enchanted. For centuries, the Venetian city state was the center of world trade, linking Western Europe with the Byzantine Empire and the rest of the known world. After the Renaissance, trade routes shifted to the Atlantic, Venice declined as a sea power. Yet throughout the 1700s, it remained Europe's most graceful city.

Today the district looks much as it did when traders unloaded silks and spices from the Orient.

The same is true of the city's splendidly painted Renaissance palaces, St. Marks' Square, and other sights.

Venice, I realized, is the antithesis of creative destruction. It exists to conserve and appreciate a past, not create a future.

But that, I realized, is exactly the point.

The city caters to a deep human need for stability and permanence as well as beauty and romance.

Venice's popularity represents one pole of a conflict in human nature: the struggle between the desire to increase material well being and the desire to ward off change and its attendant stress.

America's material standard of living continues to improve, and yet the dynamism of that same economy puts hundreds of thousands of people per week involuntarily out of work.

It's no surprise that demands for protection against the forces of market competition are on the rise as well as a nostalgia for a slower and simpler time.

Nothing is more stressful for people than the perennial gale of creative destruction. Silicon Valley is without question an exciting place to work, but its allure as a honeymoon destination has far gone largely unrecognized. (Market forces) have remained essentially unchanged since the 18th century Enlightenment.

Modern notions of political and economic freedom taken together were the beginning of the age of Enlightenment. There was a vision of a society in which individual guided by reason were at liberty to choose their destinies.

Ironically, the world Greenspan has created has limited the ability of people to create their own destinies. Freedom of speech is being stifled to silence dissident; Main Street is capitulating to Wall Street; wages are being depressed; the media spouts propaganda, burdensome taxes and increasing expenses are making home ownership and raising children prohibitively expensive; and the American government has been reduced to a banana republic.

The America the Founders established allowed people to pursue their dreams. The world Greenspan created has crushed them, limiting the options of ordinary Americans unless they wish to assume a position as a cog in the great Rothschild machine which seeks to enslave everyone.

Greenspan struggled to see why anyone would do anything if not to line his own pockets. "It's not from benevolence that the butcher, the brewer, or the baker that we expect our dinner, but from their regard to their own interest."

Spoken like a man who truly doesn't know God.

There used to be a time when bankers were prudent, fiscally responsible, and frugal, guarding the public's money and trust assiduously to ensure that the entity that entrusted them did not fall into debt or engage in wasteful spending. People, governments, and corporations lived within their means. Once Nixon took the country off the gold standard, the Federal Reserve became a printing press, ensuring that corporations could claim an unlimited amount of public funds at public expense. Deficits didn't matter, Vice President Dick Cheney once said.

Instead of seeking to provide value, the rational Enlightenment has spurred a culture of entitlement in which people seek to game the system for quick and easy profits often at someone else's expense.

Greenspan created nothing, brought no value, and had no ideas of his own. He owed his career to the financial elite. Had they not allowed him into their circles, where he became their public water carrier, he likely would have been shining shoes for a living somewhere in Brooklyn.

It never occurred to him that a butcher might wish to work at a butchery out of a desire to nourish others, to see the smiles of the faces of his customers knowing their bellies will be full that night, that his steak is of the highest quality, that he has taken care of his animals, fed them right, and treated his customers fairly. Such a butcher would sell meat at a affordable price to ensure repeat business, trust, and referrals. If he ran his business well, he would create a profit, the people would receive quality meats at an affordable price, and everyone wins.

This butcher may find joy in life on the farm and having the opportunity to be connected to the land and supporting a family established generations ago by his forefathers. The profits would follow from a job well done and a business well managed. In fact, the butcher might even become exceedingly rich.

For Greenspan, it's all about money and profits, resulting in the technocrat's latest idea to sell meat made in labs which is stripped of nutritional values but which has the texture of the real thing. It's definitely more profitable, but who wants to eat this? Nobody knows what they are eating anymore.

In globalism, Greenspan could easily be replaced with a computer who could analyze the numbers and produce recommendations faster and more efficiently that he ever could. What is the whole point of efficiently if not to serve God's creation, improve the quality of life for people? Under the system created by globalists, everything might move together in lockstep, but in the direction of tyranny to enrich a few families at the expense of everyone else.

"The accumulation of wealth previously seemed illegal and improper," said Greenspan, who characterized the idea of putting oneself first and others last as "revolutionary." The issue of how that wealth is accumulated is at question. Now raiding pension funds is considered proper. As Greenspan himself admits, he is not too bright. He's just a follower. As long as his pockets are stuffed with money, he doesn't care how it got there.

Greenspan is the poster child for a country that has lost its way. As it is written in *Matthew 6:33,* "Seek first his kingdom and his righteousness, and all the rest shall be added unto you." Put first things first. Since money wasn't the most pressing of concerns, people could focus on pursuits they enjoyed. They could live according to their values and act with integrity and good will.

What is illegal and improper is stealing everyone else's money, installing puppet governments that betray the will and the trust of the people, crashing economies for profit, waging unnecessary wars to steal another nation's natural resources, destroying families to render people dependent on the state, all to make a quick buck and become more powerful than anyone else. The American people once understood the wisdom of *1 Timothy 6:10,* that the "love of money is the root of all evil."

Greenspan believes that "if the government simply provides stability and freedom and otherwise stays out of the way, personal initiative will see the common good." However, enlightened thinking conditions one's decisions on how one can personally benefit. The common good isn't even factored into the equation. How can a government allow enterprises which are willing to flout the law and betray the public trust to have unlimited freedom to do whatever they want in their quest for profits? Freedom is only possible when people and companies self-regulate and are guided by internal core values and integrity.

V.
The Devil in The Details

After the Communist revolution had run its course in Mongolia, the Communists were in charge – until 1989, when the Cold War ended with the fall of the Berlin Wall. A Mongolian Republic was established to create the conditions needed for commerce. Rothschild was among the first to cash in....

In 1990, the North American-Mongolian Business Council (NAMBC) was established. Serving on the Board of NAMBC was Edward Story, the head of a Mongolian consulate in Texas and the Chairman of the Houston-based Pharos Energy, which is headquartered in London. Serving alongside him were numerous representatives of Oyu Tolgoi.

As could be expected, Mongolian energy interests were interested in fueling the rise of Communist China. Oyu Tolgoi was transforming Mongolia's economy into one of the fastest growing economies in the world while boosting the portfolios for those who had invested in "emerging markets."

Established during the Obama Administration, Oyu Tolgoi possesses one of the largest copper and gold mines in the world. The company was jointly owned by the Government of Mongolia and Turquoise Hills Resources (THR), whose director is Peter Griffin, Acting CEO of N.M. Rothschild & Sons.

THR owns a controlling interests in the Rothschild-affiliated Rio Tinto, which launched a thermal coal plant in Tavan Tolgoi to power the Oyu Tolgoi copper mine. The Mongolian people were outraged and demanded to know why concessions were being given to foreign investors and "members of around two dozen influential families with ties to both the ruling Mongolian Democratic party and the Mongolian People's Party (who) stand to benefit" through their ownership of shares in the Hong Kong-listed Mongolian Mining Corporation," the Associated Press reported.

Then in a surprise move, in February of 2018, the Mongolian Government terminated Rio Tinto's contract to power the Oyu Tolgoi mine in China. A domestic supplier was sought in its place.

Rio Tinto then invited three state-owned Chinese firms,

including Power Construction Corp, China Machinery Engineering Corp, and Harbin Electric International to submit bids to build the Oyu Tolgoi power station for $1.5 billion, with Oyu Tolgoi already spending $100 million a year to import electricity from China.

In December of 2018, Rio Tinto signed an agreement with Oyu Tolgoi and the Government of Mongolia for a coal plant majority owned by Oyu Tolgoi, with both controlled by Rothschild.

Another interesting character who serves on the NAMBC Board is James Wagenlander, who has been credited with creating "tighter bonds the United States is enjoying with Mongolia."

Wagenlander apparently didn't have to take the civil service exam to join the diplomatic corps. Instead, he opened up a Mongolian Consulate in Denver, Colorado, and then appointed himself Honorary Consul. He's a lawyer who specializes in Native American law.

Wagenlander has apparently not established a website for his law firm, though he has been credited with helping Mongolians rewrite their petroleum law and representing Mongolian companies in legal disputes with American companies. Thanks to his efforts, Mongolian herdsmen have been brought to Denver to meet the demand created by "a shortage of workers."

As a founder of a Sister Cities committee that links Denver, Colorado with Ulaanbaatar, the capitol of Mongolia, Wagenlander has pursued "shared economic interests" in areas of mining, tourism, and agriculture.

Denver is now the number one destination in the United States for Mongolians, who are pursuing business and law degrees at Denver University (DU) which has established a reciprocal program that allows American students to study abroad in Mongolia.

Fulbright scholarships are now available to Mongolian students through the Fulbright Commission, which was established after World War II to foster cultural understanding between Great Britain and the United States for the purposes of restoring the latter as a vassal state to the former. The Marshall and Rhodes Scholarships were established for similar purposes.

The Senator whose namesake graces the scholarship is Sen. J. William Fulbright, a passionate supporter of the United Nations who promoted America's entry into World War II.

Wagenlander also serves on the Board of Directors of the Arts

Council of Mongolia-United States alongside William Jenkins, Chair of the Zorig Foundation who worked for the Department of Defense, the Department of Energy, and the Atomic Energy Commission; and Andy Finch, the organization's chief lobbyist.

While Denver was opening its doors to Mongolia, the public noticed strange artwork at the Denver International Airport with Marxist titles like "a struggle for human liberation." Another mural entitled "humans destroying nature and themselves through destruction and genocide" inspired so much public disgust and outrage that it had to be removed. The murals gracing the terminals appeared to depict Armageddon as if signaling that Denver was the location of Hell on Earth. In keeping with Rothschild/Mongolian-inspired themes, stone gargoyles were erected to guard the baggage claim area while a devil horse greeted travelers entering the airports.

At a time in which the United States was facing severe budgetary shortfall, the Arts Council is pursuing "federal, state, and local government advocacy, grassroots campaigns, policy development, and national coalition building efforts with cultural, civic, and private sector organizations with the goal of influencing public policies."

What kind of lobbying does an Arts Council need to do, if not just shore up public funds to support artists in their creativity? The Arts Council seems to approach philanthropy a little differently than one might expect. The organization takes credit for the CREATE (Comprehensive Resource for Entrepreneurs in the Arts to Transform the Economy) Act (S.650), which was introduced by Senator Tom Udall a member of the Udall dynasty which helped facilitate settlements to Indian tribes which Udall staffers claimed as clients once they left Capitol Hill to work as lobbyists. CREATE "supports the creative economy and art entrepreneurs." Sounds benign. How does the legislation propose to do this exactly? By enlisting the Department of Commerce, the Department of Agriculture, and FEMA "to ensure expenses of self-employed workers are eligible for disaster assistance" so that they can repair or replace tools damaged or lost in the event of a disaster."

The legislation also sought to "identify and meet unmet needs in the community through artistic activities" and secure support for "partnerships with local governments and nonprofits in the economic planning of local governments." The legislation also requires the Department of Homeland Security (to) adjudicate petitions for nonimmigrant visas for aliens with extraordinary ability or achievement, artists, and entertainers within 14 days after receiving them."

Another organization affiliated with the Arts Council, the Zorig Foundation was established in 1998 as a nonprofit organization in honor of Zorig Sanjaasuren who led Mongolia's transition from a Soviet satellite state to a republic in 1990. Zorig established the legal environment for a market economy so that Mongolia could join the global economy. In 1998, Zorig was poised to become Mongolian Prime Minister but was assassinated before he took office. His sister, Oyum, who was working in the private sector in London, returned to Mongolia to claim the seat in his place.

The Mongolians have certainly made a splash in Denver. According to *The UB Post,* an English-language tri-weekly newspaper *The UB Post,* which is published in Ulaanbaatar, the Mongolians won the gold medal at the Breckenridge International Snow Sculpture Championship for their sculpture of a roaring lion. "When (a mentor and disciple) chant with the lion's roar, we can take courageous actions to win over our problems, make our dreams a reality, and awaken others to their goal potential by teaching them to practice Buddhism," *The World Tribune* reported.

The Breckenridge International Snow Sculpture Championship also awarded Mongolians first prize for a sculpture entitled "Mongolian Warriors," which the *UB Post* described as "life-like 13th century warriors and their horses striding out of a solid 20-ton block base of snow," resembling those who had slashed and burned their way through Central Asia, killing people and conquering civilizations before setting their sights on Christendom.

VI.
We, The People

As a direct descendant of the Pilgrims and Daughter of the American Revolution, I am familiar and supportive of the traditions and values upon which the United States was founded. I believe those values have been passed onto me.

I was surprised by the extent to which we the people have been lied to. I have always revered the Founding Fathers and been proud of my ancestry, to have descended from the people who established the United States. I was dismayed to discover that the great American experiment was sabotaged from the very beginning. A centuries old plan for China to rule the world under a hierarchical structure in which the few ruled the many has been in the making long before the country was even established.

Most of us have been oblivious to the dynamics in play as we have happily gone about our lives until the problem has simply become too big to ignore; we can see that our freedoms are being curtailed and that corruption has gotten out of hand.

What can we do?

First, we must educate ourselves and each other. Spread the truth so that we the people can be empowered with information. We need to understand how we got to point in history so that forge proper solutions.

Second, we must get back to our Judaeo-Christian roots. We have seen the consequences of flouting God's law. If America is to be great again, then the people must again be good. Only a virtuous people can truly be a free people – and this involves, restoring integrity to all levels of society – and demanding lawful, ethical conduct from our leaders – as culture is determined from the top down.

Third, even though our republic was compromised from the beginning, the basic structure of our republic was sound. We simply need honest people, those serving in the interests of the people, serving in government and in other leadership positions.

Fourth, the influence money has on government must be curtailed, if not eliminated altogether. Even though lobbying is a form of free speech, the system was established to provide carrots and sticks to force elected officials to serve private shadow interests over the interests of the people.

Issues of concern to this nation should receive a public airing so that the people and our elected officials can weigh in on the merits of decide whether proposed policies are truly in the interests of the people and the nation. Decisions should be made accordingly.

Fifth, the size of government needs to restrained and budgets need to be brought under control, with money spent for basic government services and public concerns, not on endless, wasteful crony contacts.

Sixth, the corporations that dominate the marketplace should be fully audited and as needed, dismantled. Many are simply the result of multi-generational public pillaging, public betrayal, and monopolistic practices. A few families control most, if not all, major corporations through interlocking boards of directors.

Seventh, we should address the legitimacy of our leaders, many of whom are serving foreign interests as a result of the undue influence of money in politics and other forms of corruption. The power resides with the Rothschilds, Vatican, and British Monarchy, but their legitimacy has been lost.

The United States was founded of, by, and for the free people under God. Queen Elizabeth I had the legal rights to colonize the territory. While the Vatican and Catholic Monarchs tried to curtail Protestant settlements, the Vatican's authority was illegitimate. As a result the Vatican and Catholic Monarchs simply could not legitimately make the claims that they did and therefore what they established can be undone.

The global elites' claim to power has been built upon a house of cards. They have misrepresented who they are, misapplied and broken laws, violated the Constitution, and committed crimes against humanity – and so the power they hold is illegitimate. They can only retain what they have through intimidation, peer pressure, propaganda, and forcing their will through the channels they have created to project their power. We have to understand how we got here and then reclaim our rights, power, and voices as sovereign, free people.

The so-called elites have robbed the people of their wealth, livelihoods, and inheritance. They have destroyed cultures and cherished traditions. It's incumbent upon us to reconnect with the traditions and values of our forefathers and mothers.

Plans to restore wealth and power to the people have apparently been underway for two decades now, through Nesara Gesara. I don't what is taking so long beyond to say that what was done has taken centuries – so undoing the damage requires patience and vigilance on our part. Also, I don't think the elites will go quietly into that good night. Their power and reach is extraordinary, impacting every aspect of our lives. They have ruthlessly pursued their agenda for generations and surely don't want to give up what they have worked so hard to get nor do they wish to face judgment – from God, the people, and the courts.

Remember, God is ultimately in control.

Made in the USA
Monee, IL
19 August 2021